"A bold and thought-provoking exploration of the future of finance, a cutting- edge guide to understand the complexities of the rapidly evolving fintech landscape!! The author's passion for harnessing technology to drive financial inclusion is very inspiring and evident in this book."

– **Ms. Shubha Naresh Bhambhani,** *Additional Director General, Department of Telecommunications Ministry of Communication & IT, GoI, New Delhi*

"With easy examples and real-world insights, it helps readers understand the basics and apply them in everyday business decisions. A perfect guide for those who don't come from a finance background but want to make smarter choices at work."

– **Dr. Narain,** *Professor of Finance, Faculty of Management Studies, University of Delhi*

I0885557

Contemporary Finance

This book presents an up-to-date account of contemporary themes and topics in finance. It explores the world of finance from a fast-changing and developing finance perspective.

Lucid, accessible, yet comprehensive, the volume discusses:

- Financial system with its constituents and instruments;
- Recent trends and approaches in value-added and strategic management;
- Current laws and legislations in the domain of taxation – direct and indirect;
- Emerging concepts and practices of digital finance, known as 'fintech'.

Presenting current global trends and real-world cases in finance and richly illustrated with tables, figures and learning tools, this volume will be indispensable for individuals, business managers and management students pursuing courses related to contemporary finance and financial management. It will also be an important resource for executive and management development programmes (EDPs & MDPs) as well as professionals, corporates, entrepreneurs, government officials, academicians and researchers.

Sandeep Goel is a Senior Professor of accounting and finance, and corporate governance at Management Development Institute (MDI) Gurgaon, India. He holds two doctorates, one in finance; and another in accounting, from the Faculty of Management Studies, University of Delhi. He completed his bachelor's degree with honors and master's degree in commerce with specialisation in finance from Shri Ram College of Commerce and the Department of Commerce, Delhi School of Economics, University of Delhi, respectively. He has three decades of industry and academic experience across various organisations and institutions of repute, including the Shri Ram Group, the University of Delhi and MDI Gurgaon. He sits as an Independent Director on the Board of Machino Plastics Ltd., Gurugram, a Suzuki JV. He is a visiting professor at the Faculty of Management, University of Lodz, Poland, and Aix-Marseille Graduate School of Management – IAE Aix-Marseille University, France. He is a management trainer and consultant to organisations like Maruti Suzuki, Canara Bank, JK Tyre, PFRDA, NPCI, IRS, ITS, FIA Business School (Brazil), Bata, Encore, Federal-Mogul Goetze (India) Ltd., SOS Village International, Cairns India, National Banking Institute (Nepal), Druk Holdings (Bhutan), UltraTech Cements, ONGC and many more. He is a prolific writer and has authored more than 15 books and published over 100 research articles and cases in national and international journals of repute. He has been conferred with the Award for Excellence in Teaching, 2023–24, 2015–16 and Award for Excellence in Research, 2015–16 at MDI.

Foundations of Finance
Series author: Sandeep Goel
is a Senior Professor, Management Development Institute (MDI) Gurgaon, India

This series presents the foundations of financial knowledge in a lucid and accessible format. The books in the series deal with critical themes in financial literacy and proficiency today, such as financial accounting, cost accounting, corporate finance, contemporary finance, forensic accounting, fraud analytics, and fraud risk management. Each volume in the series deals with updated expert insights, current global trends, and real-world cases in finance and is richly illustrated with tables, figures, and learning tools. The individual books in the series will be indispensable for individuals, business managers, and management students pursuing undergraduate and postgraduate courses in finance. They will also be important resources for executive and management development programmes (EDPs & MDPs) as well as beginners and professionals interested in a short refresher course on finance and financial management.

Contemporary Finance
Sandeep Goel

Contemporary Finance

Sandeep Goel

Routledge
Taylor & Francis Group
LONDON AND NEW YORK

Designed cover image: Getty Images

First published 2026
by Routledge
4 Park Square, Milton Park, Abingdon, Oxon OX14 4RN

and by Routledge
605 Third Avenue, New York, NY 10158

Routledge is an imprint of the Taylor & Francis Group, an informa business

British Library Cataloguing-in-Publication Data
A catalogue record for this book is available from the British Library

ISBN: 978-1-041-21226-3 (hbk)
ISBN: 978-1-041-22011-4 (pbk)
ISBN: 978-1-003-73017-0 (ebk)

DOI: 10.4324/9781003730170

Typeset in Sabon
by Apex CoVantage, LLC

Contents

Figures

Tables

Preface

Finance plays a critical function in economies and continues to evolve in practice, complemented by research, policy and regulation. The scope and reach of finance, with the changing times, have advanced in nature and practice. I take this opportunity to share with everyone the contemporary topics in the field of finance. This edition reflects the cutting edge of current trends and practices in finance, both nationally and internationally. The book provides helpful new approaches, expanded coverage and enhanced practicality, anchored by a state-of-the-art integrated learning process in the subject of finance.

Objective

The book deals with questions, like:

- What could be the business and personal implications of financial markets operating in the country?
- What decisions must managers make to manage the business operations for value-based management?
- What are the financial challenges of operating and reviving a business organisation?
- How can the technology be digitally imbued into finance to manage personal wealth and business affairs?
- How can taxes be planned at personal and corporate levels to ensure sound tax administration?

Organisation of the book

The book has been divided into five parts with ten chapters in total. It has been logically sequenced to facilitate better connectivity and learning among the readers. Most chapters are self-contained and can be read independently of the others.

Part I, 'Financial markets' discusses the constituents of *financial place constituents and instruments, mutual funds and forex market mechanics* with currency and country risks.

Part II, 'Value-based management', deliberates value-creating business decisions at the economic and human levels.

Part III, 'Strategic finance', covers two key chapters on the strategic issues in finance of *corporate restructuring and corporate governance.*

Part IV, 'Digital finance', delves into the concept and application of *fintech* in daily individual and business lives.

Part V, 'Taxation', deals with the taxation of individuals and businesses. It covers both direct and indirect taxation, in particular, *income tax and Goods and Services Tax (GST).*

I sincerely hope that the readers will find this book truly valuable in terms of its quality and presentation. Any constructive comments and suggestions for future improvement of the book are highly appreciated and welcome at *sandeepgoel1810@gmail.com.*

Happy learning!

Acknowledgements

I wish to thank God Almighty for everything in life! The work would be incomplete if I did not acknowledge my parents' contribution. They have been a constant source of inspiration for me and have always stood by me through thick and thin. My wife provided her unstinting support and encouragement in completing the book. My daughter, Maanya, is my soul, whose smile always keeps me going in life.

I am also thankful to the entire team of Routledge, New Delhi, including Dr. Shashank Sinha, Mr. Yogesh Srivastava and Ms. Anvitaa Bajaj for their tremendous support and wholehearted cooperation at all stages of publication of this book.

My sincere thanks are also due to Ms. Shubha Naresh Bhambhani and Professor Narain for their valuable support and endorsements to the book.

Last, but not the least, I gratefully express my gratitude to the following fellow academic colleagues and professional associates for providing their invaluable advice and inputs for the enrichment of the book.

- **Dr. Brian P. Miller,** *Professor of Accounting, Warrington College of Business, University of Florida, US*
- **Dr. Robert C. Rickards,** *Professor of Accounting, German Police University, Münster, Germany*
- **Dr. Maciej Turała,** *Vice Dean for International Relations, University of Lodz, Poland*
- **Mr. S.S. Sharma,** *IAS Retd., Former Secretary, Government of India, Gurugram*
- **Dr. J. P. Singh,** *Former Professor of Finance, Department of Management Studies, Indian Institute of Technology Roorkee*

- **Mr. Aditya Jindal,** *Chairman cum Managing Director, Machino Plastics Ltd., Gurugram*
- **Dr. Niti Nandini Chatnani,** *Professor of Finance, Indian Institute of Foreign Trade, New Delhi*
- **Dr. Sonam Chawla,** *Associate Professor of Organizational Behaviour, O.P. Jindal Global University, Sonipat*
- **Dr. Vishakha Bansal,** *Assistant Professor of Finance & Control, Indian Institute of Management Shillong*
- **Dr. Ajay Kumar,** *Assistant Professor, Bharati Vidyapeeth Institute of Management & Research, New Delhi*

Abbreviations

AD	authorised dealer
ADR	American depositary receipt
AMC	asset management companies
AMFI	Association of Mutual Funds in India
AMT	alternate minimum tax
API	application programming interface
AUM	assets under management
B2B	business to business
B2C	business to client
BIS	Bank for International Settlements
BoP	balance of payments
BSE	Bombay Stock Exchange
CAT	catastrophic bond
CBDT	Central Board of Direct Taxes
CCIL	Clearing Corporation of India Ltd.
COD	certificate of deposit
CP	commercial paper
CSR	corporate social responsibility
DR	depositary receipt
ELSS	equity-linked savings schemes
EmFi	embedded finance
FDI	foreign direct investment
FEDAI	Foreign Exchange Dealers' Association of India
FEMA	Foreign Exchange Management Act
FERA	Foreign Exchange Regulation Act
FII	foreign institutional investors
FMC	Forward Markets Commission
FMCG	fast-moving consumer goods
FOREX	foreign exchange
GDR	global depositary receipts
G-Secs	government securities
GSFC	Gujarat State Fertilizers & Chemicals Ltd. (formerly Gujarat State Fertiliser Company)

GSM	Global System for Mobile Communications
GST	Goods and Services Tax
GSTIN	GST identification
GSTN	Goods and Services Tax Network
HUF	Hindu undivided family
HUL	Hindustan Unilever Ltd.
HDFC	Housing Development Finance Corporation
IASB	International Accounting Standards Board
ICD	inter-corporate deposit
IFC	International Finance Corporation
IOCL	Indian Oil Corporation Limited
M&A	mergers and acquisitions
MAT	minimum alternate tax
MCA	Ministry of Corporate Affairs
MD	managing director
MNC	multinational corporations
MV	market value
NAPA	National Anti-Profiteering Authority
NAV	Net asset value
NIM	new issue market
NSE	National Stock Exchange of India Limited
OECD	Organisation for Economic Co-operation and Development
PfOF	payment for order flow
PFRDA	**Pension Fund Regulatory and Development Authority**
PSU	public sector undertaking
PV	present value
SEBI	Securities and Exchange Board of India
Sensex	Sensitive index
SGST	State Goods and Services Tax
SIDBI	Small Industries Development Bank of India
SIP	systematic investment plan
SLR	statutory liquidity ratio
SWIFT	Society for Worldwide Interbank Financial Telecommunications
SWM	shareholders' wealth maximisation
TAN	tax deduction and collection account number
T-Bill	treasury bill
UTI	Unit Trust of India
WACC	weighted average cost of capital
WDM	wholesale debt market
WTD	whole time director

Part I

Financial markets

1 Financial place constituents and instruments

The financial system is an economy's foundational engine for economic expansion. Through the mobilisation of savings and the channeling of investments into various sectors, it represents the collection of interconnected financial constituents of various markets, institutions, instruments, services and mechanisms that facilitate the process of capital formation. In the years following independence, the Indian financial system has experienced significant development and expansion in a number of areas. The post-liberalisation era (post-1991) has seen both a quantitative expansion and a diversification of economic activities.

Financial markets: overview

The financial market is a place where buyers and sellers come together and participate in the trade of securities, such as equities, bonds and derivatives. They provide the necessary linkage between the savers and investors, and help them in the exchange of their assets.

The classification of financial markets is discussed below.

I. Based on the nature of securities

(a) *Money market*: It refers to the market for short-term funds, that is, funds with a maturity of up to one year.
(b) *Capital/stock market*: It refers to the market for long-term funds, that is, funds with a maturity of more than one year.

DOI: 10.4324/9781003730170-2

II. Based on the timing of issue

(a) *Primary market*: It is a market that refers to the first-time issue of securities, that is, 'Initial Public Offering (IPO)'.
(b) *Secondary market*: It is a market that refers to the trading of existing securities.

Figure 1.1 presents the financial markets and their constituents.

Financial regulatory institutions

The financial system in India is regulated by the Government of India at the central level in the field of banking, insurance, capital market, commodities market and pension funds. These government regulatory bodies are responsible for governing the financial system through policy-making, supervision, monitoring and controlling the activities of the financial markets.

The key regulatory institutions for the Indian financial markets are:

- Banking Sector – *Reserve Bank of India (RBI)*
- Stock Market – *Securities and Exchange Board of India (SEBI)*

I. Other regulatory institutions in the Indian financial system are given below

- Insurance Sector – *Insurance Regulatory and Development Authority (IRDA)*
- Commodities Market – *Forward Markets Commission (FMC)*
- Pension Funds – *Pension Fund Regulatory and Development Authority (PFRDA)*

1. Reserve Bank of India

The Reserve Bank of India is the Central Bank of India with its head office in Mumbai. It was established on 1 April 1935 in accordance with the provisions of the Reserve Bank of India Act, 1934. It is responsible for regulating the banking system of the country. It plays a major role in regulating and controlling

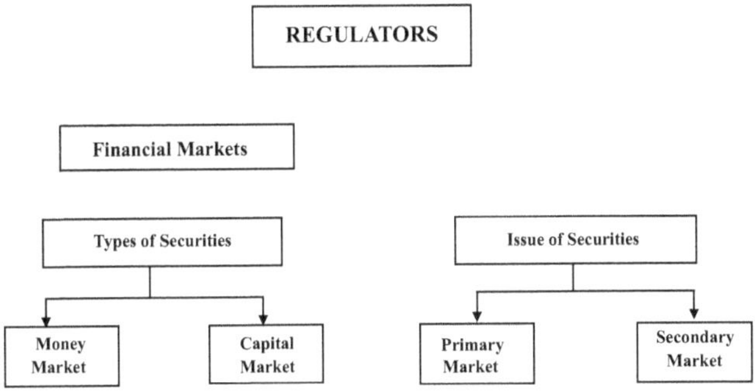

Figure 1.1 Indian financial markets.

the Indian money market. The intervention of the RBI is varied – curbing a crisis situation by reducing the cash reserve ratio (CRR) or infusing more money into the economy.

Tools of monetary control

RBI uses its 'monetary policy' for balancing the economy by one or more of the following key tools of monetary control:

(i) *Bank Rate* – It is the rate of interest charged by the central bank on the loans and advances to a commercial bank.

(ii) *Repo Rate* – It is the rate at which banks can acquire funds from the RBI by selling the securities and at the same time agreeing to repurchase them at a later date at a predetermined price. This is a short-term measure used for regulating the position of money in a bank.

[So, borrowing against securities is categorised under 'repo rate', and simple borrowing is categorised under 'bank rate'.]

(iii) *Reverse Repo Rate* – It is the rate paid by the RBI to the banks on borrowing of funds by the RBI.
(iv) *Cash Reserve Ratio (CRR)* – It refers to the cash that banks are required to maintain with the RBI as a certain percentage of their demand and time liabilities (DTL). It is a type of regulatory cash reserve with the RBI.
(v) *Statutory Liquidity Ratio (SLR)* – It refers to the liquid reserve which is required to be maintained by the banks in the form of cash and cash deposits.

2. *Securities and Exchange Board of India*

SEBI is the regulatory body that regulates securities markets in India. It was set up under the SEBI Act, 1992. It is entrusted with the responsibility of protecting the interests of investors in securities. Its functions extend to the issuance of capital and transfer of securities, in addition to controlling the activities of all intermediaries and persons associated with the securities market. It has full autonomy and authority to regulate and develop an orderly securities market.

Markets based on types of securities

Financial markets, as mentioned in the initial part, based on 'the nature of securities', are classified into *money markets* and *capital markets*.

I. Money market

A money market is a market where short-term debt instruments (with a maturity of less than one year) are traded. It refers to that segment of the financial market that enables the exchange of short-term funds and earns returns. It plays an important role in banks' liquidity management and the transmission of monetary policy. The major participants in the money market in India are the RBI and commercial banks. The Indian money market has seen exponential growth since globalisation in 1992.

The following are the 'money market instruments' and they are presented in Table 1.1.

1. *Call money*

Call money is the money lent by a bank that is repayable on demand. Therefore, the 'call market' is the most liquid market. The loans made in this market are of the shortest term: overnight. If it exceeds 1 day and extends up to 14 days, it is called 'notice money'. It is basically an interbank market, where banks facing a short-term cash crunch borrow funds from the cash surplus banks to maintain their CRR and make payments.

2. *Treasury bills (T-bills)*

Treasury bills are short-term government securities issued by the RBI on behalf of the central government. They are risk-free instruments and hence yield low returns. They are traded in both the primary and secondary markets. There are three types of treasury bills issued through auctions, namely, *91-day, 182-day and 364-day.*

They are issued at a discounted price, which is less than their face value, and redeemed at full. So, the difference between the purchase price and the maturity value is the interest earned by the buyer of the instrument.

3. *Commercial paper (CP)*

Commercial paper is a short-term, unsecured debt instrument issued by corporate and financial institutions at a discounted price, like T-bills. These are issued at a discount and redeemed at face value. The rate of interest is market-driven and depends on the current liquidity position and the creditworthiness of the issuing company. They have a fixed maturity period ranging from seven days to one year.

4. *Certificates of deposit (COD)*

A certificate of deposit is a short-term bank deposit, wherein a certificate is issued by a bank that entitles the bearer to receive interest. The certificate bears the maturity date, fixed rate of interest and the value. These deposits by the banks range from seven days to one year. The returns on certificates of deposit are higher than T-bills because they carry a higher level of risk.

5. *Discounted bills*

Bills of exchange are a short-term, negotiable and liquidating instrument with low risk. They are issued by the seller (drawer) to the buyer (drawee) for the value of the goods delivered, which can be encased with the bank for a fee. The maturity period of the bills varies from 30 days to 90 days or longer, depending on the credit extended in the industry.

6. *Inter-corporate deposit*

Inter-corporate deposits are usually unsecured inter-corporate loans. Corporate institutions with surplus funds lend to other companies. Since the cost of funds for a corporate is much higher than for a bank, the rates of such deposits are higher than other markets.

The following table presents the comparative picture of these instruments.

II. Capital market

The capital market is a market for long-term financial instruments. These long-term instruments include company shares, government bonds and corporate bonds. It is the major source of financing fixed investments, in contrast to the money market, which is the institutional source of working capital finance. The main participants in the capital market are corporate organisations, foreign institutional investors, mutual funds, insurance companies and retail investors.

Table 1.1 Money market instruments

	Instruments	*Maturity*	*Major participants*
1.	Call money	Overnight	Banks
2.	Notice money	2 to 14 days	
3.	Treasury bills	91, 182 and 364 days	Banks, foreign institutional investors, insurance companies and other non-bank entities
4.	Commercial paper	Minimum 7 days	Financial institutions
5.	Certificate of deposit	Minimum 7 days	Banks
6.	Bills discounting	Need based	Banks, insurance companies, mutual funds
7.	Inter-corporate deposit	Flexible	Corporate

The capital market in India has come a long way in the past decade and a half in terms of economic reforms, making India one of the world's largest equity markets. With around 7,000 companies listed on the stock exchanges and 20 million shareholders, India has emerged as a large investor base in the world after countries like the USA and Japan.

The 'capital market instruments' are discussed below.

1. *Owned instruments*

(I) EQUITY SHARES

Equity shares are those shares that do not carry any special or preferential rights in the payment of annual dividends or repayment of capital. They do not have a fixed rate of dividend, and their dividends are paid out of the residual profits left after paying interest on debentures and dividends on preference shares.

Similarly, equity shareholders are paid at the time of winding up of the company, after all debts and preference shareholders have been paid off. Therefore, equity shareholders are called the 'real risk-takers'. But they enjoy full voting rights in the management affairs of the company.

(II) PREFERENCE SHARES

Preference shares are those shares that carry certain special or preferential rights in the payment of dividends and repayment of capital as compared to equity shareholders.

They are paid a fixed rate of dividend, but they do not carry voting rights. Unlike equity shares, they have a fixed maturity date.

> *Preference shares* are called **hybrid security** because they are a mix of debt and equity. Like equity, they get dividends, and like debt, they get a fixed rate of dividend and have a fixed maturity.

Preference shares can be further classified into various types:

(a) **According to redemption**

- (i) **Redeemable preference shares:** They are refundable during the lifetime of the company.
- (ii) **Irredeemable preference shares:** They are issued for perpetuity.

(b) **According to convertibility**

- (i) **Convertible preference shares:** They are convertible into equity shares after a specified period of time.
- (ii) **Non-convertible preference shares:** They are not convertible into equity shares.

(c) **According to dividend payment**

- (i) **Cumulative preference shares:** Here dividend gets accumulated and paid in total if not paid in a specific year.
- (ii) **Non-cumulative preference shares:** They do not have a cumulative dividend advantage.

(III) DEPOSITORY RECEIPTS (DRS)

These are owned securities of domestic companies issued in a foreign country in its currency. Depositary receipts commonly represent a foreign equity, but can also be issued to represent ownership of preferred stock, debt or warrants. They are as follows:

(a) **American Depositary Receipts (ADRs)**
These depositary receipts are issued by non-US companies to raise capital in the US equity market from US investors. These investors can invest in international stocks without having to purchase ordinary shares.

(b) **Global Depositary Receipts (GDRs)**
GDRs are similar to ADRs; the only difference is that ADRs represent depository receipts issued in the US, whereas GDRs are depository receipts issued outside the US.

2. *Borrowed instruments*

(I) GOVERNMENT SECURITIES (G-SECS)

They refer to government and semi-government debt securities issued by the RBI and are also known as gilt-edged securities. These are risk-free securities; therefore, they offer the most suitable investment opportunity from a safety point of view.

> A *government security* is a debt obligation of the central government to fund its fiscal deficit. These instruments are tradable and are issued either by the central government or by the state government. These securities are offered for short-term as well as long-term.
>
> The 'short-term instruments' with a maturity of less than one year are called *treasury bills*, discussed earlier, whereas 'long-term instruments' with a maturity of one year or more are called *government bonds* or *dated securities.*

(II) DEBENTURES/BONDS

Debentures or bonds are known as creditorship securities because debenture holders are the creditors of a company. A debenture is a document or certificate issued by a company under its seal as an acknowledgement of its debt for a fixed term.

They carry a fixed rate of interest which is payable every year, irrespective of profits. Debenture holders do not have any voting rights.

Debentures can be further classified into the following types:

(a) **According to security**

- (i) **Secured debentures:** These are secured against the assets of the company.
- (ii) **Unsecured debentures:** These are simple debentures and have no security.

(b) **According to maturity**

- (i) **Redeemable debentures:** These are repaid within the lifetime of the company.
- (ii) **Irredeemable debentures:** These are issued for perpetuity. Nonetheless, if the company has to wind up, then it must repay these debenture holders.

(c) **According to convertibility**

- (i) **Convertible debentures:** These are convertible into shares after a specified period of time.
- (ii) **Non-convertible debentures:** These are not convertible into equity shares.

Zero-coupon bonds

'Zero-coupon bonds' do not have a specified interest rate. They are issued at a substantial discount but redeemed at full. The interest is the difference between the face value and the issue price. Therefore, they are also called 'deep discount bonds'.

Special bonds

- **Catastrophic bond (CAT bond):**
  - (i) These are bonds that have their performance linked to some catastrophic incident, such as a flood, storm, earthquake, etc.
  - (ii) If there is a calamity during the period of investment, no interest or principal will be paid to compensate the issuer for the loss.
  - (iii) If no calamity occurs during the period of investment, a higher return than other investments of the same tenure and risk profile will be received.

    It is basically a combination of a 'vanilla bond' and an 'insurance product/cover for the issuer'. It may be positioned as the securitisation of insurance risk.

    Example: **Disney Land** *issued CAT bonds, while setting up the*

    amusement park in Japan, with their performance linked to earthquakes

- **Masala bonds:** These are bonds issued outside India but denominated in Indian Rupees, rather than the local currency of that country. Masala is an Indian word that translates to 'spices'. The term was used by the International Finance Corporation (IFC) to represent the culture and cuisine of India. For foreign investors, rupee-denominated bonds are attractive as these will give them a higher interest rate compared to the standard interest rate prevailing in their markets.

The first Masala bond was issued by the World Bank-backed IFC in November 2014, when it raised 1,000 crore bonds to fund infrastructure projects in India.

In July 2016, Housing Development Finance Corporation (HDFC) raised 3,000 crore rupees from Masala bonds and thereby became the first Indian company to issue Masala bonds.

In August 2017, Indian Oil Corporation Limited (IOCL) became the first PSU in India to issue Masala bonds worth USD 300 million, which were listed on the London Stock Exchange (LSE). The bonds had a maturity of 10 years and were offered at a coupon rate of 4.375%.

(III) PUBLIC DEPOSITS

Public deposits refer to the deposits received by a company from the public as loans or debts. The companies prefer public deposits because these deposits are cheaper than bank loans. The investors invest in them as the interest on these deposits is more than the interest given by banks and post offices.

Public deposits can be further classified into the following categories:

(i) **Cumulative fixed deposits:** Here, the interest accumulates with the principal so as to earn higher returns when compared to a non-cumulative plan. They pay interest on maturity.
(ii) **Non-cumulative fixed deposits:** They pay off the interest earned on investment on a regular basis (half-yearly basis or annual basis).

(IV) TERM LOANS

Term loans are long-term loans provided by the central and state-level financial institutions to business firms. Some of the prominent financial institutions are IFCI Ltd., Small Industries Development Bank of India (SIDBI) and State Finance Corporations (SFCs).

Table 1.2 differentiates between various instruments of finance.

Table 1.2 Distinction between equity shares, preference shares and debentures

S. No.	*Basis*	*Equity Share*	*Preference Share*	*Debenture/ Loan*
1.	Type	Ownership	Ownership	Borrowing
2.	Rate of Return	Variable	Fixed	Fixed
3.	Repayment	Last	Second	First
4.	Voting Right	Yes	No	No
5.	Dilution of Control for Company	Yes	No	No
6.	Maturity	Perpetual	Fixed	Fixed
7.	Tax Deductible	No	No	Yes

Markets based on issue of securities

Financial markets based on 'the timing of issue of securities' are classified into primary markets and secondary markets.

I Primary market

A primary market is one in which new issues of a security, both debt and equity, are sold to initial buyers. It is also called the 'new issue market (NIM)'.

The process of capital formation occurs in the NIM as it supplies additional funds to the corporate directly. It does not have any physical setup like a stock market and is recognised by the services rendered by various institutions to the buyers and sellers of securities.

> In the *primary market*, when securities are exclusively offered to the existing shareholders, it is called 'right issue', and when it is issued to selected institutional investors as opposed to the general public, it is called 'private placement issue'.

II Secondary market

The secondary market, or 'stock market' as it is commonly called, is a market for old securities. It has a physical existence and is located in a particular geographical area in the form of 'stock exchanges'.

> **Stock exchanges**
>
> Stock exchanges are marketplaces where buyers and sellers come together to trade in a firm's shares and other securities. The buying and selling on an exchange is only open to its affiliates and brokers. The two leading stock exchanges in India are the BSE and the NSE, along with regional stock exchanges and others.

BSE (Bombay Stock Exchange) is the oldest stock exchange in Asia (established in 1875) and the first in the country to be granted permanent recognition under the Securities Contract Regulation Act, 1956. It has played a pioneering role in the development of the Indian securities market. Its Sensitive Index (Sensex) is the benchmark equity index that reflects the health of the Indian economy.

NSE (National Stock Exchange) was set up by financial institutions to provide access to investors from all across the country on an equal footing at the behest of the Government of India in November 1992 as a taxpaying company, unlike other stock exchanges in the country. On its recognition as a stock exchange under the Securities Contracts (Regulation) Act, 1956, in April 1993, NSE commenced operations in the Wholesale Debt Market (WDM) segment in June 1994. The Capital Market (Equities) segment commenced operations in November 1994, and operations in the Derivatives segment commenced in June 2000. NIFTY is its pioneer equity index.

Other markets

Besides the above, a new financial market has come up over the last two decades in India, that is, the *derivatives market.*

I. Derivatives market

Derivatives were introduced in India in 2000. They can be used both for hedging (protecting oneself against financial risks) and for speculation.

'Derivatives' are instruments whose value is derived from the price of some underlying asset, like securities, commodities, bullion, currency, interest level, stock market index and so forth. *For example*, a derivative of Tata Motors share will derive its value from the share price (current value) of some other company.

The common types of derivatives are as follows.

1. *Forwards*

A forward contract is a contract between two parties, where settlement takes place on a specific date in the future at today's pre-agreed price. Forwards represent the obligation to make a transaction at a set point in time in the future. They have a limitation of being informal in nature.

2. *Futures*

A future is a contract between two parties to buy or sell an asset in the future at a specific price. A future contract is a 'formal forward contract'. They are traded in an exchange.

> **Example**
>
> Ajay sells the futures contract of Reliance Industries Ltd. stock to Mac. The agreed price is Rs. 900, quantity is 100 shares and the expiry date is after one month. After a month, the price goes up to Rs. 950, then, irrespective of the market price of the stock, Ajay would make the delivery to B at Rs. 900.

3. *Options*

An option gives the contract holder the right to buy or sell on a specified date in the future – but they are under no obligation. The pre-decided price for the exchange of the asset here is called the 'strike price'.

There are two types of options: call and put.

(a) **Call option:** It gives the buyer the right but not the obligation to buy a certain quantity of the underlying asset at a given price on or before the specified date in the future.
(b) **Put option:** It gives the buyer the right but not the obligation to sell a certain quantity of the underlying asset at a given price on or before the specified date.

Example

In the above example of 'Ajay and Mac', 'the call option' gives Mac the *right*, but not the *obligation*, to purchase shares of Reliance at Rs. 900 at any point in the next month. The 'put option' is the opposite of the call option.

Thus, A 'futures contract' gives the buyer the obligation to purchase a specific asset, and the seller to sell and deliver that asset at a specific future date, whereas an 'option contract' gives the buyer the right, but not the obligation to buy (or sell) a certain asset at a specific price at any time during the life of the contract.

2 Mutual funds

The breadth and depth of the Indian financial system have increased astronomically over the past few decades. As mutual funds offer market returns at a lower risk than direct investments in the securities market, they have also risen to prominence and become a significant source of income for retail investors. A wide range of services provided by mutual funds is unavailable to investors who make direct investments in securities. Since the Indian economy was liberalised in 1991, a significant number of asset management companies (AMCs) have established themselves. These consist of bank-sponsored businesses, joint ventures (including those with foreign entities), private sector businesses and public sector businesses like Unit Trust of India (UTI).

What are mutual funds?

A **mutual fund** is a pool of money mobilised from numerous investors and invested on their behalf in the securities market. The returns from such investments, in terms of both dividends and capital appreciation, net of incidental expenses, accrue to the investors.

Each unit of a mutual fund represents the unit holder's proportionate ownership in the fund's total holdings. The investors of mutual funds are known as *unit holders*. The companies that operate the mutual funds are known as *asset management companies* (*AMCs*). The mutual fund process is depicted in Figure 2.1.

DOI: 10.4324/9781003730170-3

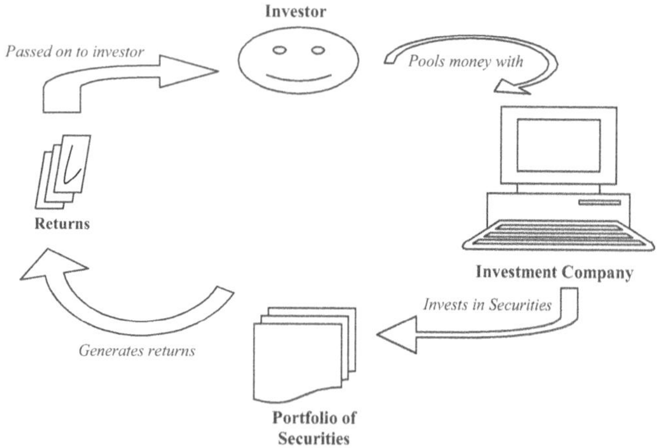

Figure 2.1 Mechanism of mutual funds.

Growth of mutual funds

Mutual funds in India began in 1963 with the setting up of the public sector undertaking UTI. UTI was set up with the twin objective of mobilising household savings and investing the funds in the capital market for industrial growth. UTI monopolised the mutual funds industry in India for more than two decades.

During 1987–1993, some other public sector organisations entered into the Indian mutual funds industry, such as *SBI (1987), Canara Bank (1987), LIC (1989), Punjab National Bank (1989), Indian Bank (1989), GIC (1990) and Bank of India (1990).*

After liberalisation in 1992, the government allowed the setting up of AMCs by private enterprises. That led to the establishment of AMCs in the private sector by Indian corporate, foreign and joint venture companies as well.

Presently, there are 44 AMCs as per the list of the Association of Mutual Funds in India (AMFI).[1]

Types of mutual funds

The categorisation of mutual funds is depicted in Figure 2.2 and explained thereafter.

I. Based on structure

Based on the structure, mutual funds can be classified as 'close-ended' or 'open-ended'.

(a) **Close-ended funds:** These funds have a pre-specified life and are redeemable at the end. These are listed on the stock exchanges and traded like stocks. So, if an investor wishes to sell the holdings or buy into such a fund before the maturity, it can be done in the stock exchange where the units are listed. *Reliance Equity Fund is an example of a well-known close-ended mutual fund.*

(b) **Open-ended funds:** These funds are irredeemable and open for investment and redemption throughout the year. Unlike close-ended funds, they are traded at the 'net asset value'

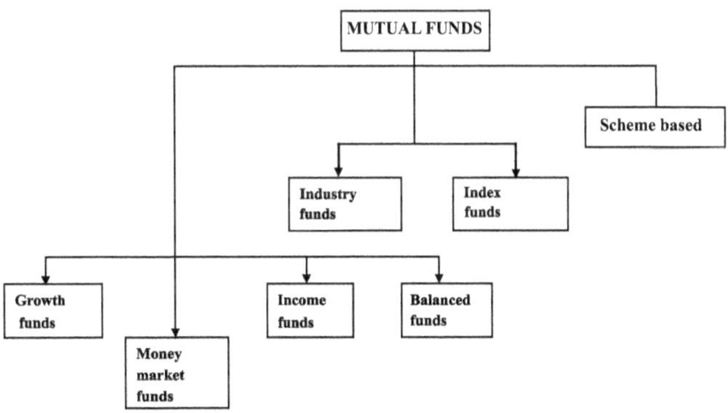

Figure 2.2 Classification of mutual funds.

(NAV) of the fund held by the AMC. That's why, in an open-ended scheme, the number of outstanding units varies on a daily basis. *Examples: UTI Dividend Yield and Axis Short Term Fund.*

Net asset value

The NAV of a fund is the sum total of the market value of the assets (securities) that comprise its portfolio, net of any liabilities at that time.

$$\text{NAV of a unit} = \frac{\text{Market value of funds(total assets) - Market value of total liabilities.}}{\text{Number of units outstanding}}$$

Example: Innovative mutual fund held Rs. 10,00,000 worth of securities, Rs. 2,00,000 of cash and Rs. 5,00,000 of liabilities on the closing day. The units outstanding were 1,00,000. What is the NAV?

$$\begin{aligned} \textit{Solution}: \text{NAV} &= (\text{Rs.}10{,}00{,}000 + 2{,}00{,}000 - 5{,}00{,}000)/1{,}00{,}000 \\ &= \text{Rs. } 7 \end{aligned}$$

II. Based on investment objective

Based on investment objective, mutual funds may be classified as follows:

(a) **Growth funds:** These funds predominantly invest in equities. They aim to grow faster than other funds, so there is usually a higher risk. They focus more on growing the value of the fund by re-investing rather than on paying out dividends.
(b) **Income funds:** These funds are primarily a debt fund. They invest in securities that pay a fixed rate of return, like *government bonds and corporate bonds.* They aim to provide returns on a regular basis, mostly through the interest that the fund earns.
(c) **Balanced funds:** These funds invest in a mix of equities and fixed income securities.

Therefore, they are riskier than fixed income funds, but less risky than pure equity. A typical balanced fund might have a weight age of 60% equity and 40% fixed income. *Example: Balanced HDFC Children's Gift-Inv Fund.*

(d) **Money market funds:** These funds invest in short-term fixed income securities, such as *treasury bills, commercial papers and certificates of deposits.* They are relatively safer investments, but have a lower return than other mutual funds. They are basically meant for liquidity.

III. Based on special schemes

Based on other factors or special schemes, mutual funds can be categorised as follows:

(a) **Industry-specific funds:** These funds are industry-specific. It could be fast-moving consumer goods (FMCG), pharmaceuticals or banking. It can extend to even geographic sectors. *For example,* an MNC fund invests in multinational or transnational companies.
(b) **Index funds:** These funds invest in a specific set of stocks of an index like the BSE Sensex or the NSE Nifty. *For example*, let us assume that a sample index consists of three Stocks, Stock A, Stock B and Stock C, in the proportions of 50%, 30% and 20%. An index fund with a corpus of say Rs. 100,000 will invest Rs. 50,000 in Stock A, Rs. 30,000 in Stock B and Rs. 20,000 in Stock C.

The value of the mutual fund will go up or down as the index goes up or down. Index funds typically have lower costs than actively managed mutual funds because the research put in by portfolio managers is less than in other investment decisions.

Equity-linked saving schemes

An ELSS is an equity mutual fund that is qualified for tax exemption under Section 80C of the Income Tax Act, 1961. It offers the twin advantage of capital appreciation and tax benefits. It comes with a lock-in period of three years.

ELSS funds not only save tax under Section 80C but also give the opportunity to earn high returns from the equity market. Moreover, compared to other tax-saving options, ELSS has the shortest lock-in period of three years. *Example: Axis Long Term Equity Fund (G).*

Importance of mutual funds

Mutual funds provide the benefits of a diversified portfolio and expert management to a large number of investors, particularly small investors. They offer the following advantages:

1 **Small investment:** Mutual funds are a boon for small investors, as it is less expensive to invest in a mutual fund. The investment amount in mutual fund units can be as low as Rs. 100.
2 **Diversification of risk:** The risk is diversified in mutual fund investments, as it is not an investment in one stock but a bundle of stocks. It automatically brings diversification to the investor's portfolio with a wide variety of securities.
3 **Professional management:** Mutual funds are managed by professionals who have a better knowledge of market behaviour. So, with mutual funds, the investors get the added advantage of experienced professional management of the portfolio.
4 **Low cost:** The cost of managing mutual funds by the companies is very low. Mutual funds usually hold numerous securities; therefore, the actual level of fees can vary. But the expense ratio of mutual fund investments is relatively low.
5 **Liquidity:** Mutual funds are liquid investments that can be sold anytime. Investors can plan out their cash requirements with these investments. The price per unit at which you can redeem units is known as the fund's NAV.
6 **Convenience:** The investor can purchase or sell fund shares directly from a fund or through a broker, by any medium, physically or electronically.
7 **Tax relief:** The mutual funds also provide a tax advantage to investors. ELSS mutual funds provide tax relief under

Section 80C of the Income Tax Act, 1961. Like shares, long-term capital gain is levied, and up to Rs 1 lakh a year is tax-exempt.

Systematic investment plan

A SIP involves investing a fixed amount in a mutual fund at regular intervals, monthly or quarterly, over a period of time, thereby averaging out the cost of investing and yielding the benefit from the 'power of compounding'. It is similar to an investment in a recurring deposit account in a bank.

In SIP, the investors do not have to worry about the market timing as it is governed by the principle of 'rupee cost averaging' (RCA).

Reference

1 Association of Mutual Funds in India, https://www.amfiindia.com/know-about-amfi (accessed on 18 September 2023).

3 Forex market

The international financial system provides the framework within which foreign exchange rates are determined, international trade and capital flows are accommodated, and balance of payments (BoP) adjustments are made. The forex market is an integral part of the international financial system. The increase in world trade and the reduction in capital controls have led to tremendous growth in the foreign exchange market over the years. The Indian forex market has seen tremendous growth since liberalisation in 1991. Since the independence of India in 1947, the four-decade-old, fixed exchange rate system replete with severe import and foreign exchange controls was replaced with a less regulated, 'market-driven' exchange rate arrangement in 1993.

Forex market!

The forex market, or 'foreign exchange market', is the market that brings the participants across the globe together to buy, sell, exchange and speculate on currencies. It comprises banks, financial companies, central banks, investment management firms, hedge funds and retail forex brokers and investors. The currency market is considered to be the largest financial market in the world, processing trillions of dollars' worth of transactions each day.

I. *Features*

1 *OTC market*: The forex market is an 'over-the-counter market' (OTC market). This means that there is no single market or physical stock exchange but an electronic market where

DOI: 10.4324/9781003730170-4

trading takes place. The traders sit in the offices (foreign exchange dealing rooms) of major commercial banks around the world and communicate with each other through telephones, telexes, a satellite communication network, SWIFT and other electronic means of communication. All transactions happen here via phone or electronic network.

> 'SWIFT' is an acronym for 'Society for Worldwide Interbank Financial Telecommunications'.
>
> It is a cooperative society owned by about 250 banks in Europe and North America and registered as a cooperative society in Brussels, Belgium. It is a communications network for international financial market transactions that links effectively more than 11,000 financial institutions throughout the world that have been allotted bank-identified codes.

1 *24-hour market*: It is a market that operates 24 hours a day at the global level. It spans all the time zones of the world and enables a trader to offset a position created in one market using another market. The major market centres are London, New York and Tokyo.
2 *Participants*: The major participants of the forex market are central banks, commercial banks, financial companies and retail investors. Central banks are the biggest players in the forex market, involved in the massive buying and selling of currency to fix exchange rates through their open market activities, not for mere profit reasons, but rather for policy matters.

> **Structural framework of forex market**
>
> The market for foreign exchange can be divided into the 'retail market' and the 'wholesale market'.
>
> In the *retail market*, tourists and travellers exchange one currency in the form of currency notes or traveller's

cheques to meet their foreign exchange requirements. The average transaction size is very small. The retailers buy or sell foreign currency from banks and other institutions that are authorised to deal in foreign exchange.

The *wholesale market* is often called the *interbank market*. The participants in this market are commercial banks, investment banks, corporate houses and central banks. The average transaction size is very large (deals may be in millions of US dollars or other currency).

3 *Risk*: The participants in this market trade in currencies of various countries and generate profits for their organisations. In this process, these organisations get exposed to 'foreign exchange risk'.
4 *Process*: In a 'forex trade', you buy one currency while simultaneously selling another; that is, you are exchanging the sold currency for the one you are buying. Currencies are traded in pairs, like the euro-US dollar (EUR/USD) or US dollar/Japanese yen (USD/JPY).

The global foreign exchange turnover as available on 27 October 2022 is given in Table 3.1.

Foreign exchange market in India

The forex market in India can be discussed with regard to its growth, structure, process and role of CCIL under the following heads:

I. *Growth*

The growth of the forex market in India is discussed as follows.

(a) *Before 1991*: Traditionally, the Indian forex market was highly regulated. Till liberalisation in 1991, the government exercised absolute control on the exchange rate, export-import policy and FDI (foreign direct investment) policy. The Foreign Exchange Regulation Act (FERA), 1973, strictly controlled

Table 3.1 OTC foreign exchange market turnover 'Net-net' basis,[1] daily averages in April, in billions of US dollars

Instrument	*2010*	*2013*	*2016*	*2019**	*2022*
Foreign exchange instruments	3,973	5,357	5,066	6,581	7,508
Spot transactions	1,489	2,047	1,652	1,979	**2,107**
Outright forwards	475	679	700	998	**1,163**
Foreign exchange swaps	1,759	2,240	2,378	3,198	**3,810**
Currency swaps	43	54	82	108	**124**
Options and other products[2]	207	337	254	298	**304**
Memo:					
Turnover at April 2022 exchange rates[3]	*3,542*	*4,727*	*4,851*	*6,446*	***7,508***
Exchange-traded derivatives[4]	*144*	*145*	*115*	*127*	***152***

Source: Bank for International Settlements (BIS)- Triennial Central Bank Survey.[1]

* Revised data

1 Adjusted for local and cross-border inter-dealer double-counting (i.e., 'net-net' basis).

2 The category 'other FX products' covers highly leveraged transactions and/or trades whose notional amount is variable and where a decomposition into individual plain vanilla components was impractical or impossible.

3 Non-US dollar legs of foreign currency transactions were converted into original currency amounts at average exchange rates for April of each survey year and then reconverted into US dollar amounts at average April 2022 exchange rates.

4 Euromoney Tradedata; Futures Industry Association; The Options Clearing Corporation; BIS derivatives statistics. Foreign exchange futures and options traded worldwide.

all foreign exchange-related activities. Under the Act, all forex earnings by companies and residents had to be reported and surrendered (immediately after receiving) to the RBI at a rate decided by the RBI.

(b) *After 1991*: The new Foreign Investment Policy announced in July 1991 declared automatic approval for Foreign Exchange in India for 34 industries. These industries were designated with high priority, up to an equivalent limit of 51%. The foreign exchange market in India is regulated by the RBI through the Exchange Control Department.[4]

Post-liberalisation, the Government of India liberalised the foreign exchange policy in the form of the Foreign Exchange Management Act (FEMA) 1999. FEMA expanded the list of activities in which a person/ company can undertake forex transactions. Through FEMA, the government liberalised the export-import policy, limits of FDI and FII (foreign institutional investors) investments, cross-border M&A and fundraising activities.

> The Foreign Exchange Management Act, 1999, is a regulation for the foreign exchange market in India. The RBI regulates the Indian foreign exchange market through the Exchange Control Department.

II. Structure

The foreign exchange market in India consists of three interdependent segments or tiers.

a. *RBI and authorised dealers (ADs)*: The first is an apex segment consisting of transactions between RBI and authorised dealers. ADs are usually commercial banks authorised by the RBI to deal in foreign exchange. The exchange rates are set by the RBI. It facilitates exchange rate movements in tune with international developments as a residual partner rather than as an active market participant.
b. *Interbank market*: This is the major segment of the forex market in which the ADs deal with each other. More than 70% of the trading in foreign exchange takes place in the interbank market. The big commercial banks are the 'market makers' in this market, as they are willing to buy or sell foreign currencies at the rates quoted by them up to any extent.

   The trading is regulated by the Foreign Exchange Dealers' Association of India (FEDAI), a self-regulatory association of ADs. The market consists of 99 ADs (mostly banks and others, including financial institutions) as of August 2023.[2]
c. *Retail market*: In this segment, ADs deal with their corporate clients and other retail customers. The retail market deals in currency notes and traveller's cheques for tourists. It also consists of moneychangers and foreign exchange brokers.

III. Centres

The leading foreign exchange market in India is Mumbai. Other forex centres include Kolkata, Chennai and New Delhi. As a result of the RBI's efforts to decentralise exchange operations and develop broader-based exchange markets, new centres of the forex market have emerged, such as Bangalore and Ahmadabad.

IV. CCIL – Role in clearing process

The Clearing Corporation of India Ltd. (CCIL) was set up in April 2001 to provide guaranteed clearing and settlement functions for transactions in money, government securities, foreign exchange and derivative markets.[3] It was set up on the initiative of the RBI to mitigate risks in the Indian financial markets. Since 2001, as India's first centralised clearing and settlement house for the financial sector, it facilitates settlement of both debt and forex transactions.

Types of foreign exchange markets

Depending upon the time elapsed between the transaction date and the settlement date, foreign exchange transactions can be categorised into the following.

I. Spot market

'Spot market' is the market where transactions for the exchange (purchase and sale) of currencies take place two days after the date of the contract.

> *For instance,* if the contract is made on Monday, the delivery should take place on Wednesday. If Wednesday is a holiday, the delivery will take place on the next day, that is Thursday. The rupee payment is also made on the same day the foreign currency is received.
>
> Similarly, if the contract is made on Wednesday, then the delivery should take place on Friday. If Friday is a holiday, the delivery will take place on Tuesday of the following week if Saturday and Sunday are bank holidays, as they are at most of the financial centres.

The exchange rate for spot delivery is called the *spot exchange rate* and is denoted by S(). *For example*, S(Rs/USD) = Rs. 65.10/USD is the relationship between rupees and dollars, which says that one dollar is equivalent to Rs. 65.10.

II. Forward market

The 'forward market' is the place where the transactions for the exchange of currencies take place at a specified future date after the spot date. The forward transaction can be for delivery one month, two months, three months and so forth.

This may be done to secure against adverse movements in currencies (a *hedging transaction*) or to trade a currency (a *speculative transaction*).

III. Swap market

It is a combination of a spot and a forward transaction. The term 'swap' implies a temporary exchange of one currency for another with an obligation to reverse it at a specific future date. Swaps are two-way deals, one deal involving a buy and the other involving a sell, at different times, but one has to cancel the other.

The following are the categories of swaps:

(i) *Spot-forward swap*: In this swap, one deal is done in the spot market and another in the forward market, that is, one buys in the spot and sells in the forward or vice versa. If the buy is in spot and sell in the forward, it is called a 'swap-in'.

> *For example,* if an exporter expects to receive USD 5,000 two months hence but needs money at present, he goes to a bank and asks for a swap. He buys USD 5,000 in the present and sells them in the forward at the agreed price. Conversely, if sell is in the spot and buy is in the forward, it is called a 'swap-out'.

(ii) *Forward-forward swap*: Here, both the deals are in the forward, that is, one buys two months forward and sells three months forward, each deal cancelling the other or vice versa.

For example, an exporter expects a receipt of USD 2,000 after three months and has to pay the suppliers after two months. So, the exporter contacts a bank for a swap. The bank agrees to the swap and sells USD 2,000 two months forward to the exporter and buys USD 2,000 three months forward from him at the agreed rates.

Foreign exchange quotations

A 'quotation' is the amount of currency that is exchanged for a unit of another currency. When a currency is quoted, it is done in relation to another currency, so that the value of one is reflected through the value of another.

The following are the types of forex quotations.

I. Two-way quotations

Typically, the quotation in the interbank market is a two-way quotation. It means the rate quoted by the bank will indicate two prices, *one* at which it is willing to buy the foreign currency, and *the other* at which it is willing to sell the foreign currency. 'A two-way quote includes both bid and offer rate'.

The buying rate is also known as the 'bid rate', and the selling rate as the 'offer rate'.

The difference between these rates is the gross profit for the bank and is known as 'the spread'.

For example, a Delhi bank may quote its rate for the US dollar as: USD 1 = Rs. 68.10/15. More often, the rate would be quoted as 10/15, since the players in the market are expected to know the 'big number', that is, Rs. 68. In the given quotation, there are two rates, that is, the bank is prepared to buy USD at Rs. 68.10 and sell at Rs. 68.15.

II. Direct quotations

The exchange quotation that gives the price for the foreign currency in terms of the domestic currency is known as 'direct quotation'.

Here, the *unit of foreign currency* is kept constant, and its value is expressed in terms of variable domestic currency.

> *For example:* USD 1 = Rs. 68.10
> GBP 1 = Rs. 86.50

III. Indirect quotations

The exchange quotation that gives the quantity of foreign currency per unit of domestic currency is known as 'indirect quotation'.

Here, the *unit of home currency* is kept constant, and its value is expressed in terms of the foreign currency.

> *For example:* Rs. 100 = USD 1.47
> Rs. 100 = GBP 1.15

References

1 Bank for International Settlements. 'Triennial Central Bank Survey of OTC Foreign Exchange Turnover', https://www.bis.org/statistics/rpfx22_fx.pdf (accessed on 25 September 2023).
2 Member Banks/FIs, https://fedai.org.in (accessed on 25 September 2023).
3 The Clearing Corporation of India Ltd., www.ccilindia.com/ABOUTUS/ Pages/CompanyProfile.aspx (accessed on 10 August 2016).
4 Foreign Exchange Market in India. 'Indian Economy – India Netzone', www.indianetzone.com/38/foreign_exchange_market_india.html (accessed on 8 August 2016).

Part II

Value-based management

4 Economic value added

'Value creation' is the ultimate objective of any corporate organisation. The most successful organisations understand that the purpose of any business is to create value for its customers, employees, investors and, most importantly, its shareholders. There are many companies that are not managed to their full potential value. Their managers act as value destroyers with their misguided actions. 'Managing for value creation' provides the basis for a comprehensive and integrated *value-based management system* that not only helps in evaluating the business performance for all the stakeholders but also enables the management to take sound business decisions for future growth.

What is value creation?

'Value creation' is a corporation's **raison d'être**, the ultimate measure by which it is judged. Debate has focused on what is the most appropriate type of value for the corporation to create. Is it:

- *The value of the company in the stock market ?*
- *The value shown in its balance sheet (the accounting or book value of its assets minus its liabilities)?*
- *The value based on its expected future performance – profits or cash?*
- *None of these?*[1]

> From the *financial perspective*, value is said to be created when a business earns revenue more than expenses, that is, when its return on capital exceeds the cost of capital.

DOI: 10.4324/9781003730170-6

Economic value added: the shareholders' value

The shareholders are the most important stakeholders of a company, being the owners of the company. Therefore, the main emphasis of the management is on creating value for shareholders.

I. Traditional measures

Traditional approaches to measuring 'shareholder value creation' have used parameters such as *earnings capitalisation, market capitalisation* and others.

1. Market price

In the 1990s, the measure which was prominently used for analysing shareholders' value was the *company's market price*. The presumption was that shareholders look for capital gains from their investments. But a measure based on stock market value is subject to the same wild fluctuations as the market itself. In a rising tide, all boats are raised. But when the macroeconomic changes force up-markets, it does not mean that the value of every company in that market rises. The markets are moved by sentiment that has little to do with the underlying value of individual corporations.[1]

2. Earnings per share

The limitation of market value, as discussed earlier, was evident in the form of the dotcom frenzy at the end of the 1990s. So, a group of scholars favoured *earnings per share (EPS)* as the real measure of shareholders' value. But the accounting measures are not carved in stone. They can (and do) differ from country to country and have their own set of accounting limitations. They are not free from the biases of the management.

II. Economic value added measure

A measure developed to overcome these problems is called EVA (economic value added). It is the professedly managed innovation in the field of internal and external performance measurement.

Stern Stewart, a UK-based consulting firm, unveiled EVA in 1990, but its origin as economic profit dates back to the early 1900s. *EVA is the financial performance measure that captures the true economic profit of an enterprise.* This is the reason why EVA has been successfully employed in nearly 400 companies worldwide, including well-known firms as Coca-Cola, Siemens and Sony.[2]

1. *EVA computation*

This is the measure of output (taken as operating profit after tax and some other adjustments) less input (taken as the annual charge on the total capital employed, both debt and equity). In simple terms, EVA is the profits generated by any economic entity over its cost of capital employed. If the difference between the above two parameters is positive, then the entity is said to be creating wealth for its stakeholders. A negative EVA, on the other hand, indicates the company is a destroyer of value.[2]

$$\textbf{EVA} = \textbf{Net Operating Profit after Tax (NOPAT)} - \textbf{Cost of Capital Employed (COCE)}^{*}$$

Where *NOPAT* is the profits generated from the core operations of the company.

It is calculated as:

$$\text{Profit before Tax} + \text{Non-operating items (including Interest)} - \text{Tax.}$$

Cost of Capital Employed is calculated as: Weighted average cost of debt and equity (WACC) × Average Capital employed. It is the total invested capital in the business.

Thus, the real test of the management is to generate returns higher than the investment from core activities for shareholders' wealth maximisation. According to Mr. Roberto Goizueta, the former chairman and CEO of the Coca-Cola Company and an ardent believer in the maximisation of shareholders' wealth: *Management doesn't get paid to make shareholders comfortable. We get paid to make the shareholders rich.*[3]

2. Example: How is value created?

Young India Company (YIC) is a leading software company in India. In 2023, YIC's net assets generated pre-tax operating profits of Rs. 240 million, as reported in its income statement. The corporate tax rate is 30%.

* 'Cost of Capital Employed' is also referred to as Weighted average cost of capital (WACC).

The company employed Rs. 1,000 million of capital as shown in the balance sheet for 31 March 2023. YIC's WACC is 10%.

EVA = Net Operating Profit after Tax (NOPAT) – Weighted Average Cost of Capital

(i) NOPAT = Rs. 240 million – Rs. 72 million (30 % tax amount)
= Rs. 168 million

(ii) WACC = Rs. 100 million (10% * Rs. 1,000 million)

So, EVA = Rs. 168 million – Rs. 100 million
= Rs. 68 million

YIC generated Rs. 168 million of after-tax operating profit (NOPAT) but consumed Rs. 100 million of funds in the process. Therefore, YIC generated a positive EVA of Rs. 68 million in 2023. As long as YIC continues to generate positive EVA, it will create value.

How to grow EVA?

EVA will increase if:

(a) Operating profits are increased with less capital, that is, greater efficiency of resources is there.
(b) Return on capital invested in additional projects is more than the cost of obtaining new capital; that is, profitable growth is achieved.
(c) Capital is used in activities that cover the cost of capital; that is, productive usage is done.

Case: EVA of Hindustan Unilever Limited (Sector – FMCG)

Hindustan Unilever Limited (HUL) is a leading FMCG company in India. It is a company around 100 years old in the sector in India with brands such as Dove, Lux, Lipton and Lifebuoy, among others.

The company has been following EVA for years. In HUL, the goal of sustainable long-term value creation for our shareholders is well understood by all the business groups. This can be seen in Table 4.1 and Figure 4.1.

III. Calculation of COCE

1 *Cost of debt* is taken at the effective rate of interest applicable to an 'AAA' rated company like HUL for a short-term debt, net of taxes. They have considered a pre-tax rate of 6.43% for 2021–22 (6.28% for 2020–21).
2 *Cost of equity* is the return expected by the investors to compensate them for the variability in returns caused by fluctuating earnings and share prices.

$$\text{Costofequity} = \text{Risk} - \text{freereturn equivalent to yield on long-term government bonds } (\text{taken at } 6.84\% \text{ for } 2021-22). + \text{Market risk premium } (\text{taken at } 3.68\%) \times \text{Beta variant fortheCompany, } (\text{taken at } 0.614)$$

where Beta is a relative measure of risk associated with the Company's shares as against the market as a whole.

$$\text{Thus HUL's cost of equity} = 6.84\% + 3.68\% \times 0.614 = 9.09\%$$

IV. Analysis

HUL has shown considerable improvement in EVA (from Rs. 4,258 crores in 2018 to Rs. 6,085 crores in 2020, with a decline

Table 4.1 EVA reporting of HUL

(Rs. in crores)

Particulars	*2017–18*	*2018–19*	*2019–20*	*2020–21*	*2021–22*
Cost of Capital Employed (COCE)					
1 Average Debt	0	0	0	0	0
2 Average Equity	6,181	6,668	7,227	46,890	**47,156**
3 Average Capital Employed: [1]+ [2]	6,181	6,668	7,227	46,890	**47,156**
4 Cost of Debt, post-tax %	5.21	5.77	5.25	4.70	**4.81**
5 Cost of Equity %	14.19	11.84	9.11	8.86	**9.09**
6 Weighted Average Cost of Capital % [WACC]	14.19	11.84	9.11	8.86	**9.09**
7 COCE: [3] × [6]	877	789	658	4,153	**4,289**
Economic Value Added (EVA)					
8 Profit after tax (PAT), before exceptional items	**5,135**	**6,080**	**6,743**	**7,963**	8,724
9 Add: Interest, after taxes	0	0	0	0	0
10 Net Operating Profits After Taxes [NOPAT]	5,135	6,080	6,743	7,963	**8,724**
11 COCE, as per [7] above	877	789	658	4,153	**4,289**
12 EVA: [10] – [11]	**4,258**	**5,291**	**6,085**	**3,810**	**4,435**

Source: Hindustan Unilever Limited. 2022. 'Economic Value Added', Annual Report 2021–22, https://www.hul.co.in/files/92ui5egz/production/8a1b3f103408328781a6ebf434b8e5172e4bfc91.pdf (accessed on 26 September 2023).

Note: Rs. 1 crore = Rs. 10 million.

in 2021 for known external factors. In 2022, it again showed an increasing trend). The company has been able to bring down the cost of capital (COCE) significantly in 2019 and 2020 and then maintain a steady increase to become a zero-debt company, thereby improving EVA performance.

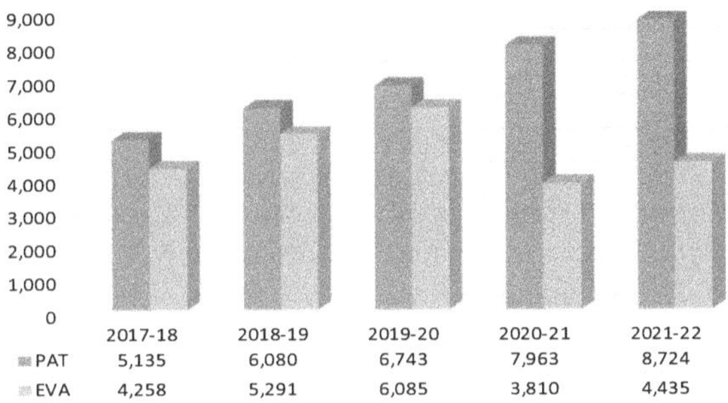

Figure 4.1 EVA trend of HUL.

Note: Rs. in crores.

Therefore, the difference between PAT and EVA is not very huge except during the past two years – a positive sign for the shareholders.

How to measure value creation? Market value added

As is known, the core objective of financial management is 'value creation'. This means that before making a business decision, managers should always ask themselves the key question: *Will the decision raise the value of their firm?*

The key question can be answered with the help of the fundamental finance principle, 'when the return on invested capital exceeds the cost of capital', that is, 'EVA'.

EVA and growth#

Goel (2012) found that the companies in India that were reporting positive EVA for the period 2004 to 2009 had grown at a much faster pace compared to the Sensex, vis-à-vis the companies reporting negative EVA.

The companies that were not reporting EVA had underperformed with respect to the Sensex.[2]

MVA framework!

EVA is directly linked to the growth of the company, and that is expressed by 'market value added' (MVA). If MVA is positive, the firm is creating real value because the market value of its capital exceeds the amount of capital invested in it. If MVA is negative, the firm is destroying the value.

The real measure of determining the value of a company is EVA with positive MVA. To find out whether the management has created or destroyed value as of a particular point in time, the *market value* of the firm is compared with its total capital (both equity and debt capital) to the amount of capital that shareholders have invested in the firm (the firm's capital employed).

$$\textbf{Marketvalue added (MVA)} = \text{Market value of capital} - \text{Capital employed}$$

I. *Example: EVA versus MVA*

Considering the earlier example of Young India Company, a leading software company in India, let us understand the implications of MVA. The company employed Rs. 1,000 million of capital as shown in the balance sheet for 31 March 2023. It consisted of Rs. 700 million of equity and Rs. 300 million of debt. The market value of that capital as on the date was Rs. 1,500 million.

$$\begin{aligned} MVA &= \textit{Market value of capital} - \textit{Capital employed} \\ &= \text{Rs. } 1{,}500 \text{ million} - \text{Rs. } 1{,}000 \text{ million} \\ &= \textit{Rs.}\ 500 \text{ million} \end{aligned}$$

So, MVA is positive with Rs. 500 million, indicating that YIC has created Rs. 500 million of real value as of 31 March 2023 with a positive EVA of Rs. 68 million.

How to estimate the market value of capital?

(i) *For publicly listed companies*: The market value of capital can be obtained from the financial markets, at least for firms whose equity and debt capital are publicly traded in the form of securities.

(i) *For private companies*: If the firm is not publicly traded, its market value is unobservable and its MVA is difficult to calculate. It can be calculated based on its estimated purchase price, that is, if someone makes an offer to buy the firm, then it could be taken based on that 'offer price'.

References

1 The Economist. 2009. 'Value Creation, "The Ultimate Measure By Which a Company Is Judged"', 20 November, www.economist.com/node/14301714# (accessed on 5 September 2016).
2 Goel, S. 2012. 'EVA Reporting in India: The Market Analogy', *Singapore Management Review*, 34 (2): 18–29.
3 Shapiro, A. 1990. *Modern Corporate Finance*. Basingstoke: The Macmillan Company, p. 333.

5 Human resource valuation

'Value creation' is a total effort-based approach to management that requires managers at all levels of the organisation to manage their firm's resources efficiently and thereby contribute to the accomplishment of the ultimate objective of maximising a firm's value. Shareholders' value creation should be compatible with other stakeholders as well, including the loyal customers, suppliers and the 'dedicated work force', that is, *human resource*. It is the most vital input on which the success and failure of the organisation largely depend. In the era of knowledge and technology, only those organisations can survive and succeed that can effectively manage their human resources. The motivated employees are the real assets of any organisation who can take it to greater heights. Therefore, their valuation and contribution to the organisation need to be recognised.

Human valuation: meaning

Human resource valuation (HRV) or human resource accounting (HRA) is a specialised branch of accounting that provides significant information about the cost, value and performance of the human resources in an organisation and helps in the effective human resource management.

Human resource accounting has been defined by the Committee on Human Resource Accounting of the American Accounting Association as *the process of identifying and measuring data about human resources and communicating this information to interested parties.*[1]

DOI: 10.4324/9781003730170-7

Human resources is one of the most important 'M' in the 4M's associated with any organisation, that is, ***money, machines, materials*** and ***men.*** But the surprising fact is that the first three are recognised and find a place in the assets side of the balance sheet of organisation.

But, the fourth 'M' (men) has universal ambiguity prevalent about its treatment in the financial statements, despite being the most important element of an organisation. The International Accounting Standards Board (IASB) and the Accounting Standards Board (ASB) in India have not been able to formulate any specific accounting standard for the measurement and reporting of human resources.

The companies that report their human resource value do so in the form of additional information in the notes and not as an integral part of the financial statements. It is like an intangible asset.

Indian Accounting Standard (Ind AS) 38 – Intangible Assets

Ind AS 38, which deals with intangible assets, states that human resources cannot be treated as intangible assets as they are not under the 'control' of the company.

Paragraph 15 of Ind AS 38 is reproduced below:

> *An entity may have a team of skilled staff and may be able to identify incremental staff skills leading to future economic benefits from training. The entity may also expect that the staff will continue to make their skills available to the entity. However, an entity usually has insufficient control over the expected future economic benefits arising from a team of skilled staff and from training for these items to meet the definition of an intangible asset. For a similar reason, specific management or technical talent is unlikely to meet the definition of an intangible asset, unless it is protected by legal rights to use it and to obtain the future economic benefits expected from it, and it also meets the other parts.*

Importance of human resource valuation

'Human resource value' is often considered a useful component of an 'enterprise value', especially in service industries, where manpower is the single largest input for generating income. In recent years, a number of companies in the information technology sector have included such valuation in their annual reports, although a number of public sector units in the manufacturing sector have been reporting these numbers for long.

The benefits of adopting HRA are manifold, as discussed below.

1 **Better decision-making.** It helps an organisation to make managerial decisions based on the availability and the necessity of human resources. The valuation of human resource provides a true insight to various stakeholders into the organisation and its future potential.
2 **Effective control.** The company can determine whether its human asset is appreciating over the years or not. This information becomes important particularly for knowledge-based industries as their success depend solely on the knowledge of the employees.
3 **Proper compensation.** This information can be used by the company internally to compare the performance and productivity of employees in various departments. Accordingly, it can decide the compensation of employees.
4 **Growth potential.** The company can identify and retain valuable employees for future growth.

To sum up, HRA helps an organisation in identifying the right person for the right job, based on the person's knowledge, skills, capabilities and experience.

Limitations of human resource valuation

Human resource valuation is not free from demerits. These are as follows:

1 **Inter-comparison difficult.** Different companies might be using different HRA models, and comparing two companies using two different models is difficult and not meaningful.

2 **Misuse of HRA.** The companies can misuse HRA to enhance their image. A company can use the assumptions in human valuation to its benefit in order to keep the values positive.
3 **Models not fool proof.** The human valuation methods are based on various assumptions, which are in themselves subjective. Hence, figures could be totally ambiguous. There could be a concern about the credibility of the numbers reported.

Human valuation methods

Various methods and models developed for valuing human resources are based on *cost or economic value of human resources*. Under these methods human resources of an organisation are translated into a common denominator, that is, money on which organisational decisions are taken. The value of human asset can be shown on a conventional balance sheet and statement of profit and loss.

These methods are discussed as follows:

1 **Historical cost method.** This method was developed by Rensis Likert. Under this method, all actual costs incurred on recruitment, training, selection and so forth are capitalised. Then, the capitalised cost is amortised (written off) over the period an employee serves in the organisation. In case the employee leaves the organisation before his expected service period, the remaining amount is written off completely in that particular year of his/her leaving the organisation.
2 **Replacement cost method.** 'Replacement cost' refers to the cost of replacing an existing employee with another employee rendering equivalent services. This method values the human resource on the basis of his replacement cost, that is, the cost of recruitment, training and development, opportunity cost for the period till the new recruit attains the same efficiency level as the old (to be replaced) employee.
3 **Opportunity cost method.** This method is used to value those employees who possess specific skills and, thus, are rare in availability. A 'bid price' is offered by the managers for acquiring such scarce employees. This bid price becomes the investment in such employees. The bid price is arrived at by calculating the actual or expected rate for capitalisation of

the potential earnings to be earned by such employees. This method has the drawback of the absence of a well-justified criterion to decide the amount of the bid.

4 **Economic value method.** Under this method, human asset is valued on the basis of the contribution they will make to the organisation till their retirement from the job. The payments made to them in the form of salary, allowances, benefits and so forth are estimated and then discounted to arrive at the present economic value of the individuals. This is also called the *Discounted net present value of future earnings* method.

The Lev and Schwartz model

The most commonly used method by Indian companies is the Lev and Schwartz model, which values human resources in the form of discounted present values of all future payments to the employees.

The Lev and Schwartz model states that *the human resource of a company is the summation of the value of all the Net present value (NPV) of expenditure on employees.*

Under this model, the following steps are adopted to determine HR value:

(a) Classification of the entire labour force into certain homogeneous groups, like skilled, unskilled, semi-skilled, etc., and in accordance with different classes and ages. *For example, at Infosys, the classification is based on software professionals and support staff* and so forth.
(b) Construction of the average earning stream for each group. *As above,* at Infosys, incremental earnings based on group/ age have been considered.
(c) Discounting the average earnings at a predetermined rate in order to get the present value of the human resources of each group.
(d) Aggregation of the present value of different groups that represent the capitalised future earnings of the concern as a whole.

$$Vr = I(t) / [(1 + r) ^\wedge (t - r)$$

Where Vr = the value of an individual r years old
I (t) = the individual's annual earnings up to retirement
t = retirement age
r = a discount rate as per the cost of capital to the company.

This model has its own limitations as well.

Human resource accounting: the industry practice

The first attempt to value human beings in monetary terms was made by Sir William Petty (1623–1687).[3] He treated human beings as an element of wealth.

For the first time, HRA was implemented in 1967 by R. G. Barry Corporation, a footwear manufacturing company in Ohio (USA).[4]

I. Indian scenario

In India, the importance and value of human assets gained momentum in the early 1990s when there was a major increase in employment in firms in service, technology and other knowledge-based sectors. In these knowledge-based firms, the intangible assets, especially human resources, contributed significantly to the building of shareholder value.

'It was first introduced in India by Bharat Heavy Electricals Ltd. (BHEL), a leading public enterprise, during the financial year 1973–74'.[5] Later it was also adopted by other leading public and private sector organisations in the subsequent years. Some of them are Hindustan Machine Tools Ltd. (HMT), Oil and Natural Gas Corporation Ltd. (ONGC), National Thermal Power Corporation Ltd. (NTPC), Associated Cement Company Ltd. (ACC), Tata Engineering and Locomotive Company Ltd. (TELCO) and Infosys Technologies Ltd. (ITL).

However, different companies adopted different models for HRV and also different discount rates and disclosure patterns, such as age-wise, skill-wise and so forth. This makes it clear that there has been no uniformity among Indian enterprises regarding HRA disclosure.

Case: human resource valuation at Infosys Technologies Ltd.

In the financial year 1995–96, Infosys Technologies (Infosys) became the first software company to value its human resources in India. The company used the 'Lev and Schwartz' model and valued its human resources assets at Rs. 1.86 billion. Infosys had always given utmost importance to the role of employees in contributing to the company's success.

Mr. Narayana Murthy, the then chairman and managing director of Infosys, said, *Comparing this figure over the years will tell us whether the value of our human resources is appreciating or not. For a knowledge intensive company like ours, that is vital information.*[6]

II. Use of the Lev and Schwartz method to value HR in Infosys

As mentioned earlier, Infosys used the Lev and Schwartz model for HRV. The evaluation is based on the present value of future earnings of employees.

1. Assumptions

The assumptions made by Infosys in the evaluation are:

(a) Employee compensation includes all direct and indirect benefits earned both in India and overseas.
(b) The incremental earnings based on group/age have been considered.
(c) The future earnings have been discounted at the cost of capital of 11.21% (previous year 10.60%).

2. *Methodology*

The methodology used by Infosys in the process is as follows:

- All the employees of Infosys were divided into five groups, based on their average age. Each group's average compensation was calculated.
- Infosys also calculated the compensation of each employee at retirement by using an average rate of increment.
- The increments were based on industry standards, and the employee's performance and productivity.
- Finally, the total compensation of each group was calculated. This value was discounted at the rate per annum, which was the cost of capital at Infosys, to arrive at the total human resources of Infosys.

The HRV figures of Infosys are given in Table 5.1 and its HRV reporting is given in Table 5.2.

Table 5.1 Human resource valuation at Infosys for 2011

in ₹ crore, unless stated otherwise

	2011	*2010*
Employees (nos.):		
Software professionals	1,23,811	1,06,864
Support	7,009	6,932
Total	**1,30,820**	**1,13,796**
Value of human resources:		
Software professionals	1,22,539	1,06,173
Support	12,566	7,114
Total	**1,35,105**	**1,13,287**
Total income(1)	27,501	22,742
Total employee cost(1)	14,856	12,093
Value-added	25,031	20,935
Net profit(1)	6,823	6,219
Ratios:		
Value of human resources per employee	1.03	1.00
Total income/human resources value (ratio)	0.20	0.20
Employee cost/human resources value (%)	11.0	10.7
Value-added/human resources value (ratio)	0.19	0.18
Return on human resources value (%)	5.1	5.5

(1) As per IFRS (audited) financial statements.

Note: Rs. 1 crore = Rs. 10 million.

Table 5.2 Balance sheet of Infosys including intangible assets as of 31 March 2011

in ₹ crore	*2011*	*2010*
ASSETS		
Current assets:		
Cash and cash equivalents	16,666	12,111
Available-for-sale financial assets	21	2,518
Investment in certificates of deposit	123	1,190
Trade receivables	4,653	3,494
Unbilled revenue	1,243	841
Derivative financial instruments	66	95
Prepayments and other current assets	917	641
Total current assets	**23,689**	**20,890**
Non-current assets:		
Property, plant and equipment	4,844	4,439
Goodwill	825	829
Intangible assets		
Brand value	40,509	36,907
Human resources value	1,35,105	1,13,287
in ₹ crore	**2011**	**2010**
Other intangible assets	48	56
Available-for-sale financial assets	23	38
Deferred income tax assets	378	346
Income tax assets	993	667
Other non-current assets	463	347
Total non-current assets	**1,83,188**	**1,56,916**
Total assets	**2,06,877**	**1,77,806**
LIABILITIES AND EQUITY		
Current liabilities:		
Trade payables	44	10
Current income tax liabilities	817	724
Client deposits	22	8
Unearned revenue	518	531
Employee benefit obligations	140	131
Provisions	88	82
Other current liabilities	2,012	1,707
Total current liabilities	**3,641**	**3,193**
Non-current liabilities:		
Deferred income tax liabilities	–	114
Employee benefit obligations	259	171
Other non-current liabilities	60	61

(*Continued*)

Table 5.2 (Continued)

in ₹ crore	*2011*	*2010*
Total liabilities	**3,960**	**3,539**
Equity:		
Share capital	286	286
Share premium	3,082	3,047
Retained earnings	23,826	20,668
Capital reserves-intangible assets	1,75,614	1,50,194
Other components of equity	109	72
Total equity attributable to equity holders of the company	**2,02,917**	**1,74,267**
Total liabilities and equity	**2,06,877**	**1,77,806**

Notes: The figures above are based on IFRS financial statements.[7]

Rs. 1 crore = Rs. 10 million.

III. Analysis

Infosys has shown human resources as an 'intangible asset' under its balance sheet of 2011, given in Table 5.2.

1 The total number of core employees increased from 1,06,864 in 2010 to 1,23,811 in 2011; an increase of 15.86%. The increase is clear in the number of both software professionals and support staff.
2 The total human resource value has shown an increasing trend from Rs. 1,13,287 crores in 2010 to Rs. 1,35,105 crores in 2011, showing an increase of approximately 20%. This is a positive sign for human resources' contribution to the company's profits.

It is evident that the human resource value has increased at a faster rate than the number of employees, indicating better productivity of employees.

References

1 American Accounting Association. 1973. 'Report of the Committee on Human Resource Accounting', *The Accounting Review*, 48 (Supplement): 169.

2 Indian Accounting Standard (Ind AS) 38. 'Intangible Assets', http://mca.gov.in/Ministry/pdf/INDAS38.pdf (accessed on 1 July 2018).
3 Suresh, R. 2006. 'Human Resource Accounting: A Behavioural Approach', *The Management Accountant*, February: 91.
4 Brummet, G.M., Flamholtz, M.C. and Pyle, C.R. 2009. 'Human Resource Accounting: A Tool to Increase Managerial Effectiveness', *Management Accounting*: 12–15.
5 Kashive, N. 'Importance of Human Resource Accounting Practices and Implications of Measuring Value of Human Capital: Case study of Successful PSUs in India', *XIMB Journal of Case Research*, 4 (2), http://home.ximb.ac.in/~jcr/cases/Case03-HRA-DEC2013.pdf (accessed on 27 August 2017).
6 Rao, A. 2014. 'Employee Participation, Valuation of Human Resources and Creation of Intangible Assets', *International Journal of Business and Administration Research Review*, July–September, 3 (6): 47, www. ijbarr.com/downloads/0111201419.pdf
7 Infosys. 2011. 'Human Resource Valuation', Annual Report 2010–11, www.infosys.com/investors/reports-filings/annual-report/annual/Documents/ AR-2011/ai_20.html (accessed on 1 October 2016).

Part III

Strategic finance

6 Mergers and acquisitions

Every organisation wants to grow over a period of time. There are two ways by which a company can grow its size: *first,* by eating the market share of the competitor; *second,* by eating the competitor itself. In other words, growth may be attained either organically or inorganically. *Organic growth* is increasing the profit base of the organisation through the capital investment process. *Inorganic growth, or external growth*, is accomplished through various business combinations, namely, mergers and acquisitions (M&A). These business combinations are an important feature of 'corporate restructuring' and have played an important role in the external growth of a number of leading companies around the world. The type of approach to be used by the organisation depends upon various factors, such as growth cycle of the business, time period, resources available and, of course, the risk factor.

Forms of business combinations

Business combinations can be categorised as follows.

I. Merger

Merger means 'combination of two things'. In a business sense, the term 'merger' refers to a fusion between two or more enterprises, which results in the emergence of a single enterprise. Such a process involves the transfer of assets and liabilities of the merging companies to the merged (combined) company. The shareholders

DOI: 10.4324/9781003730170-9

of the merging company/companies become the shareholders in the merged company.

The basic objective of a merger is to improve the operational efficiency of the merging entities. The companies that transfer their assets to the other company are termed as *transferor* or *the merging companies*, and the company to which such assets are transferred is known as *transferee* or *the merged company.*

Merger versus absorption versus amalgamation

Absorption is a merger with an existing company, where all other firms are absorbed into the surviving firm. *For example*, the absorption of Hutchinson Essar Ltd. by Vodafone Plc. Vodafone, an acquiring company (a buyer), survived after the merger, while Hutch, an acquired company (a seller), ceased to exist. Hutch transferred its assets, liabilities and shares to Vodafone.

Amalgamation/consolidation implies that all the firms are combined to form a new entity through the transfer of all their property to such a new corporation. In this case, the existing companies cease to exist; *for example*, the merger of Hero Group and Honda Motor Company Ltd. into an entirely new company called 'Hero Honda Ltd'.

The term 'merger' is used interchangeably with these terms.

II. Acquisition

An 'acquisition or takeover' refers to the acquisition of effective working control by one company over another. The control may be acquired either through the purchase of the majority of shares carrying voting rights or by controlling the composition of the board of directors of the other company. The company acquiring shares is termed the *holding company*, while the company in which the shares are acquired is termed the *subsidiary company.*

In an acquisition, two or more companies may remain independent, separate legal entities, but there may be a change in control of the companies.

Types of mergers

Mergers are of the following types.

I. Horizontal merger

This is a combination or joining of two or more firms in the same area of business. In a horizontal merger, both the merging firm(s) and the merged firm(s) produce and sell identical or similar products in the same geographic area. A merger of firms that are in direct competition with each other is called a horizontal merger.

> *For example*, the merger of Vodafone India with Idea Cellular to form Vodafone Idea Ltd. (Vi) and the acquisition of Daksh by IBM are examples of horizontal mergers.

The advantages of a horizontal merger are as follows:

- Elimination or reduction in competition
- End to price wars
- Economies of scale in operations.

II. Vertical merger

This is a combination of two or more firms involved in different stages of the production or distribution. A combination of two or more firms that fall in the same industry but operate at different stages of the production–distribution chain is termed as a vertical merger.

One example of such merger is between Time Warner Inc., a major cable operation, and the Turner Corporation, which produces CNN, TBS and other programming.

Vertical merger may take the form of 'forward' or 'backward integration'. When a company combines with the supplier of material, it is called *backward integration (merger)*, for example, a tyre manufacturer integrates with a rubber manufacturing firm. It is an upstream merger.

When a firm combines with the buyer or customer, it is known as a *forward integration (merger)*, for example, a tyre manufacturing firm combines with a two-wheeler manufacturing firm. It is a downstream merger.

The advantages of a vertical merger are as follows:

- Reduction in the cost of production
- Optimisation of resources
- Better service resulting from supply chain integration.

III. Conglomerate merger

This is a combination of two or more firms that are engaged in unrelated lines of business activity. It is a type of combination in which firm(s) established in one industry combine with other firm(s) in an unrelated industry. It generally involves diversification of business activities and, therefore, is considered to pose no threat to competition.

For example, the merging of different businesses, like the merger of a company manufacturing cement products and electronics products. The merger between the Walt Disney Company and the American Broadcasting Company is an example of conglomerate merger.

The advantages of such a merger are as follows:

- Market expansion or product extension
- Mitigation of risk.

A brief explanation of each form of combination is given in Figure 6.1.

Motives of mergers and acquisitions

The key goal of mergers and acquisitions is considered to be 'the maximisation of shareholders' wealth'. In general, mergers and acquisitions are done for the following motivations:

1 **Synergies:** This is the most common reason for a merger. The value of the new entity will be more than the combined value of the two separate companies. Generally, there are two types of synergies that are aimed for:

   - *Operating synergies*: These are the synergies that result in economies of scale due to an increase in the scale of operations of the combined firm. Such an optimal utilisation of resources brings down the cost per unit of output. Operating economies also accrue in specific management functions such as R&D, production, marketing or finance.

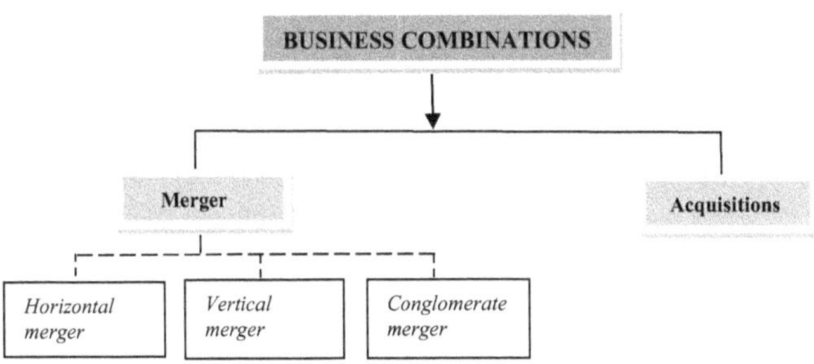

Figure 6.1 Forms of business combinations.

- *Financial synergies*: These are the synergies that increase the capacity of the combined firm to mobilise financial resources at a lower cost. They further increase the overall revenue through expansion in markets, product cross-selling and an increase in prices.

2 **Profitability:** Operational synergies enhance operational efficiency and economies of scale of the acquiring company. Duplication of resources can be avoided by the combined firm, which may bring down the cost of operations and lead to higher profits. The financial synergies can lead to access to cheaper funds (debt), reducing the overall cost of capital and giving a push to the profitability.
3 **Market power:** A horizontal merger in a small industry helps in increasing the market share. An increased market share will, in turn, give the power to influence prices. A vertical merger can also increase the market power by reducing the dependence on external suppliers.
4 **Reduction in competition:** Merging with (or acquiring) the competitors not only increases the market share of the acquiring company but also reduces its competition significantly. This reduction in competition is direct in the case of horizontal mergers and indirect in the case of vertical mergers, as the benefits of upstream/downstream integration in vertical mergers provide the combined firm a significant cost advantage over its competitors.
5 **Rapid growth:** Mergers and acquisitions are a way of achieving external growth by increasing sales through external resources.

   The companies that are in the mature phase generally prefer to grow externally. It is less risky to have external growth. M&A results in the expansion of resources, thus increasing the growth rate.
6 **Diversification:** The company can diversify easily through the M&A route. This is cheaper and less stringent than the company going through the process of entering into a new line of business single-handedly.
7 **Increase in EPS:** A merger deal is expected to have a positive effect on the company's EPS. This occurs due to an increase in the profit base of the acquiring company. An increase in

the current EPS of the company will lead to an increase in the market price of the share.

8 **Tax saving:** Merging with firms having accumulated losses allows the merged firm to set off these accumulated losses against the post-merger profits of the merged firm. The provisions under Section 72A and 72AA of the Indian Income Tax Act, 1961, allow this facility to set off and carry forward the losses against the profits of the merged entity. Such a set-off reduces the taxable income of the merged firm, resulting in tax savings for it.
9 **International presence:** International mergers and acquisitions have become more common and important in today's business world for global outreach.

Process of mergers and acquisitions

There are three important steps involved in the analysis of mergers and acquisitions.

I. Planning

The acquiring firm should review its objectives of acquisition in the context of its strengths and weaknesses and the corporate goals. This will help in identifying the product market strategies that are suitable for the firm.

Due diligence refers to the reasonable care that should be taken before entering into an agreement or a transaction. It is an investigative process or audit of a potential transaction or deal, so as to find out all relevant facts pertaining to the ensuing transaction. There are various types of 'due diligence', such as *technological due diligence, environmental due diligence, organisational due diligence, financial due diligence and so forth.*

In the context of M&A, it refers to assessing the price and identifying the financial risks involved in an M&A

deal. The decisions to merge/acquire/takeover are based on the due diligence report. Critical issues addressed by such an analysis from the perspective of the acquiring/merged firm may include the following:

(i) Value of target firm(s)
(ii) Synergies from the deal
(iii) Estimated value creation for the acquiring/merged firm from the deal and so forth

II. Search and screening

Search enables the finding of suitable candidates for acquisition. Screening shortlists the candidates from the available lot, and then detailed information about each of these candidates is obtained.

III. Financial evaluation

Financial evaluation of a merger is needed to find out the earnings, cash flows, areas of risk, the maximum price payable to the target company and the best method for financing the merger. This involves the application of different valuation methods.

M&A valuation methods

There are three main methods for business valuation. Among all the methods, the 'discounted-cash-flow' (DCF) method is the most commonly used valuation method in M&A. These methods are discussed below.

I. Asset-based – net assets method

In the case of 'privately held' companies, market information is not available. So, the *net assets method* is commonly used in these acquisitions. A comparative analysis is done of the target company with regard to its total asset size and its outstanding liabilities to determine the net purchase price.

> The total value of the assets (minus the liabilities) of the target company is computed to find out the value of the equity of its business.

Illustration 6.1: Ind Ltd. decides to acquire 100% equity of Bright Corp. Bright Corp. is a private limited company with Rs. 80 million of market value of assets and Rs. 50 million of liabilities outstanding. What is the acquisition value as per the net assets method?

Solution

Total assets of Bright Corp.	= Rs. 80 million
Less: Outstanding Liabilities	= Rs. 50 million
Acquisition Price	= Rs. 30 million

II. Income-based – discounted cash-flow method

The discounted cash-flow method in an M&A deal attempts to determine the value of the company by computing the present value of cash flows over the life of the company. It involves discounting the future expected cash flows over a forecast period and comparing them with the investment price to arrive at the decision. Basically, the NPV approach is used here, as follows, in capital budgeting decisions. If the NPV of the investment is positive, it is a viable M&A decision and vice versa.

Illustration 6.2: AB Company is considering acquiring Z Ltd. for Rs. 10 million in cash at 14% cost of capital. Z Ltd. can generate Rs. 2 million of cash inflows over the next 15 years. Using NPV, advise whether it is a viable acquisition for AB Company.

Solution:	
Initial Cash Outlay [A] =	Rs. 10 million
Present Value of Cash Inflows of Rs. 2 million = (6.142 × 2 million) [B]	Rs. 12.284 million
Net Present Value [B – A] =	Rs. 2.284 million

Based on NPV, AB Company should acquire

Z Ltd., since there is a positive NPV for this investment.

Note: 6.142 is the present value factor of annuity at 14%, 15 years.

III. Market-based – market value method

This method is popular in the case of 'publicly held' companies. Market value (MV) is presumed to reflect the public information about the company and its industry. On average, a profitable company merger's offer commands a suitable premium over the price.

Its computation involves the following steps:

1. Calculate the 'value the equity' of the firm (E): Stock price × outstanding shares.
2. Calculate the 'market value of debt' (D): Price per bond × number of bonds outstanding.
3. Calculate the value the firm (V): E + D.

Illustration 6.3: New India Ltd. is a publicly listed company with 20,00,000 shares outstanding. The market price per share is Rs. 70, and the fair market value of its debt is Rs. 10 million. What is the market value of the firm for the proposed acquisition?

Solution

Market Value of Stock (20,00,000 × Rs. 70) =	Rs. 140 million
Market Value of Debt =	Rs. 10 million
Value of the Firm =	Rs. 150 million

Enterprise value method

The enterprise value method is an extension of the market value method. The 'enterprise value' is calculated as:

'Value of equity + Value of debt – Cash and cash equivalents'

7 Corporate governance

Ever since India's biggest-ever corporate fraud and governance failure was unearthed at Satyam Computer Services Ltd. in 2008–09, the concept of good corporate governance has again come into the limelight. Corporate governance has been an important area of discussion in the whole world, particularly over the last two decades. It has emerged from obscurity into being a mainstream topic and has moved into all sections of the corporate sector and the political scene. Corporate governance is important not only from a legal point of view but also from the stakeholders' value perspective. It should be seen as practice rather than an obligation from a firm's view.

Concept of corporate governance

Corporate governance is concerned with the standards of behaviour and conduct expected from directors and other senior executives (including the financial manager) in directing and controlling the affairs of a company. Corporate governance not only defines the relationships between managers and shareholders but also includes the relationships between the board, senior executives, shareholders, other stakeholders, such as customers, suppliers and employees, regulators and the firm's auditors.

The simplest definition of corporate governance is provided by the Cadbury Report (UK): *Corporate governance is the system by which businesses are directed and controlled.*[1]

DOI: 10.4324/9781003730170-10

The Organisation for Economic Co-operation and Development

(OECD) Principles of Corporate Governance state:

> *Corporate governance involves a set of relationships between a company's management, its board, its shareholders and other stakeholders. Corporate governance also provides the structure through which the objectives of the company are set, and the means of attaining those objectives and monitoring performance are determined.*[2]

SEBI (2003) states that '[t]he aim of good corporate governance is to enhance the long-term value of the company for its shareholders and all other partners. Corporate governance integrates all the participants involved in a process, which is economic, and at the same time social'.[3]

Need for corporate governance

The necessity for having sound corporate governance arises because of the following factors:

1 **Efficient allocation of resources.** The efficient allocation of scarce economic resources is a priority. It will be achieved if companies are accountable to those who take profit or bear the loss after all other claims on the company have been met.
2 **Wide spread of shareholders.** Today, a large number of shareholders of the company are spread all over the nation and even the world; a majority of shareholders are unorganised and have an indifferent attitude towards corporate affairs. In such a scenario, it is necessary that shareholders' democracy is well implemented through a code of conduct of corporate governance.
3 **Shareholders' confidence.** Corporate scams (or frauds) in the past several years have shaken public confidence in corporate management. The need for corporate governance is, thus, imperative for maintaining the investors' confidence in the corporate sector.

4 **Societal expectations.** The society of today holds greater expectations of the corporate sector in terms of reasonable price, better quality, environmental contribution and so forth. To meet social expectations, there is a need for a code of corporate governance for the company in economic and social terms.
5 **Sound growth.** For long-term, quality growth, it is necessary that the boards of the companies carry out the affairs of the management of the company and monitor the development with good corporate governance.
6 **Globalisation.** The globalisation of the economy has driven the largest companies to access international capital markets. Frauds on a global scale have led to greater awareness of the inadequacies of governance and demand for reform in corporate practices.

Principles of corporate governance

The key fundamental principles of corporate governance are described as follows.

I. Transparency

Transparency means the 'quality of something' which enables one to understand the truth easily. In the context of corporate governance, it implies an accurate, adequate and timely disclosure of relevant information about the operating results and other information of the corporate enterprise to the stakeholders.

In fact, transparency is the foundation of corporate governance, which helps to develop a high level of public confidence in the corporate sector. To ensure transparency in corporate management, a company should publish relevant information about corporate affairs in a timely manner.

II. Accountability

Accountability is a liability to explain the results of one's decisions taken in the interest of others. In the context of corporate governance, accountability implies the responsibility of the chairman, the board of directors and the chief executive for the use of the company's resources (over which they have authority) in the best interest of the company and its stakeholders.

III. Independence

Good corporate governance requires independence on the part of the top management of the corporation; that is, the board of directors must be free from all biases so that they can take all corporate decisions objectively.

OECD principles of corporate governance

Originally developed by the OECD in 1999, then updated in 2004, the 2015 revision of the Principles of Corporate Governance addresses these and other emerging issues that are increasingly relevant. These Principles provide an indispensable and globally recognised benchmark for assessing and improving corporate governance.

The principles have been adopted as one of the Financial Stability Board's key standards for sound financial systems, and have been used by the World Bank Group in more than 60 country reviews worldwide. They also serve as the basis for the guidelines on corporate governance of banks issued by the Basel Committee on Banking Supervision.[4]

These are as follows:

- I *Ensuring the basis for an effective corporate governance framework*
- II *The rights and equitable treatment of shareholders and key ownership functions*
- III *Institutional investors, stock markets and other intermediaries*
- IV *Disclosure and transparency*
- V *The responsibilities of the board*
- VI *Sustainability and resilience*[5]

Acquisitions versus takeovers

Though acquisition and takeover have a similar connotation in corporate restructuring, 'acquisitions' basically are willingly done, whereas 'takeovers' are hostile. A 'forced' acquisition is called a takeover.

Evolution of corporate governance

I. International

1. US

The USA is known for its shareholder-oriented or market-based model of corporate governance, with features like *active institutional investors, an open market for corporate control, independent outside directors on the board, long-term equity-based compensation for executives* and *gatekeepers who monitor the process of market disclosure.*

However, scandals like Enron in 2000 generated criticism and led to substantial changes in corporate regulation through the 'Sarbanes–Oxley' (SOX) legislation.

> The Sarbanes–Oxley Act of 2002 (SOX) introduced major changes to the regulation of financial practice and corporate governance to protect investors from the possibility of fraudulent accounting activities by corporations.

2. UK

The first version of the UK Corporate Governance Code (the Code) was produced in 1992 by the 'Cadbury Committee'. In 2012, they came out with the new Code, which applies to all listed companies regardless of whether they are incorporated in the UK or elsewhere.

Presently, the corporate governance model in the UK is based on the 'UK Corporate Governance Code' 2018. This market-based approach is basically a system of 'comply or explain' (UK Corporate Governance Code) and allows the board to be flexible. The UK Corporate Governance Code is a set of principles of good corporate governance aimed at companies listed on the LSE.

It sets standards of good practice in relation to board leadership and effectiveness, remuneration, accountability and relations with shareholders.

II. India

Corporate governance was initially guided by *Clause 49* of the Listing Agreement before the introduction of the Companies Act of 2013. As per the new provision, the SEBI has also approved amendments to the Listing Agreement so as to improve the transparency in transactions of listed companies and give a bigger say to minority stakeholders in influencing the decisions of management. These amendments became effective in 2015.

1. Desirable Code of Corporate Governance – Voluntary Code by CII (1998)

Corporate governance in India gained prominence in the wake of liberalisation during the 1990s and was introduced by the industry association Confederation of Indian Industry (CII) as a voluntary measure to be adopted by Indian companies. The first major initiative was undertaken by the CII in 1998 in the form of the *Desirable Code of Corporate Governance – Voluntary Code.*

2. The Kumar Mangalam Birla Committee Report (2000)

Consequently, the second major corporate governance initiative in the country was undertaken by SEBI. In early 1999, it set up a committee under Kumar Mangalam Birla to promote and raise the standards of good corporate governance. ***In early 2000, the SEBI board ratified the key recommendations of the Birla Committee, which were incorporated into Clause 49 of the Listing Agreement of the Stock Exchanges.*** It soon acquired a mandatory status in the early 2000s through the introduction of Clause 49 of the Listing Agreement, as all prescribed companies listed on stock exchanges were required to comply with these norms.

3. The Naresh Chandra Committee report (2002)

The Naresh Chandra Committee was appointed in August 2002 by the Department of Company Affairs (DCA), under the Ministry of Finance and Company Affairs, to examine various corporate governance issues. The Committee submitted its report in December 2002. It made recommendations in terms of two key aspects of corporate governance: *financial and non-financial disclosures, and independent auditing and board oversight of management.*

4. *The N. R. Narayana Murthy committee report*

(Second report of the SEBI Committee) (2003)

With an objective to improve corporate governance standards in India, SEBI once again constituted a committee in 2002 under the chairmanship of N. R. Narayana Murthy to review the existing code on corporate governance. Some of the major recommendations of the committee primarily related to audit committees, audit reports, independent directors, related party transactions, risk management, directorships and director compensation, codes of conduct and financial disclosures.

5. *Dr. J. J. Irani Committee report (2005)*

India's corporate governance reform efforts did not cease after the adoption of Clause 49. In parallel, the review and redrafting of the Companies Act, 1956, were taken up by the Ministry of Corporate Affairs (MCA). The government constituted an Expert Committee on Company Law under the Chairmanship of Dr. J. J. Irani on 2 December 2004 to offer advice on a new Companies Bill. Based, among other things, on the recommendations of the Irani Committee, the Government of India introduced the Companies Bill, 2008, in the Indian Parliament to introduce the best international corporate practices that foster entrepreneurship and investment. *This finally became the Companies Act, 2013.*

6. *Kotak Committee report*

(Third report of the SEBI Committee) (2017)

SEBI set up a committee on corporate governance in June 2017 under the Chairmanship of Mr. Uday Kotak with a view to enhancing the standards of corporate governance of listed entities in India.

On 28 March 2018, SEBI approved many Kotak recommendations on corporate governance. The recommendations accepted without modification included *reduction in maximum number of listed entity directorships from ten to eight, expanding the eligibility criteria for independent directors and mandatory disclosure of consolidated quarterly results with effect from 2019–20.*

Corporate governance regulation in India

The Indian legal framework has, by and large, been in consonance with the international best practices of corporate governance. Broadly speaking, the corporate governance mechanism for companies in India is regulated by the following regulations.

I. The Companies Act, 2013

The Companies Act, 2013 ('New Companies Act'), replaces the erstwhile Companies Act, 1956, with its applicability still in place. The Companies Act is the principal legislation governing companies in India. It contains provisions relating to board constitution, board meetings, board processes, independent directors, general meetings, audit committees, related party transactions, disclosure requirements in financial statements and so forth.

The New Act covers corporate governance through the following provisions:

- The companies should have an adequate composition of the boards of directors.
- Every company is required to appoint one resident director on its board.
- The New Companies Act for the first time codifies the duties of directors.
- Listed companies and certain other public companies shall be required to appoint at least one woman director on their board.
- A class action suit was introduced for minority shareholders.
- The New Companies Act mandates the following committees to be constituted by the board for the prescribed class of companies:

- *Audit committee*
- *Nomination and remuneration committee*
- *Stakeholders relationship committee*
- *Corporate social responsibility committee*

Corporate social responsibility (CSR) obligations

India is the only country in the world with codified corporate social responsibility (*CSR*) obligations. The Companies Act, 2013, requires specified companies to spend at least 2% of the average net profits made during the three immediately preceding financial years on prescribed CSR activities. This provision operates on a 'comply or explain' basis, and the board of directors must provide an explanation in the directors' report if the company does not spend the requisite amount on CSR.

This requirement is applicable to companies that satisfy the following criteria:

(i) A net worth of at least Rs. 5 billion during any financial year
(ii) A turnover of at least Rs. 10 billion during any financial year
(iii) A net profit of at least Rs. 50 million during any financial year.

Every company that fulfils the above threshold requirements must constitute a corporate social responsibility committee, formulate a CSR policy and make recommendations on CSR to the board. The CSR activities must be performed within India and are not permitted to be for the exclusive benefit of the company's employees or their family members.

II. SEBI's Listing Obligations and Disclosure Requirements (LODR) Regulations, 2015

Presently, the Corporate Governance framework for Listed Companies in India is governed by SEBI (LODR) Regulations, 2015, as amended from time to time. It replaced the governance regime under Clause 49. In addition, Companies are also bound by the standard listing agreement of BSE/NSE.

> ***Revised Clause 49:*** SEBI is a regulatory authority having jurisdiction over listed companies and which issues regulations, rules and guidelines to companies to ensure protection of investors. *SEBI has amended the Listing Agreement with effect from 1 October 2014 to align it with the New Companies Act.*
>
> Revised Clause 49 (2014) and the First Clause 49 (2005) of the Listing Agreement can be said to be a bold initiative towards strengthening corporate governance among the listed companies. This clause intends to put a check on the activities of companies in order to save the interests of the shareholders

Broadly, **the above regulations** of corporate governance provide for the following:

1. Board of directors

The board of directors shall have an optimum combination of executive and non-executive directors, with not less than 50% of the board of directors comprising non-executive directors.

(a) Where the *chairman* of the board is a *non-executive director*, at least one-third of the board should comprise independent directors, and in case the *chairman is an executive director*, at least half of the board should comprise independent directors.

(b) If the non-executive chairman is a promoter of the company or is related to any promoter or person occupying management positions at the board level or at one level below the board, at least one-half of the board of the company shall consist of independent directors of such number of minimum independent directors, as prescribed.

Independent directors

An independent director is any non-executive director who possesses relevant expertise and integrity and is in no way related to the company.

2. *Audit committee*

The audit committee to be set up comprises a minimum of three directors as members, two-thirds of whom shall be independent.

3. *Disclosure requirements*

Periodical disclosures relating to the financial and commercial transactions, remuneration of directors and so forth need to be made by the company to ensure transparency.

4. *CEO/CFO certification*

The CEO and the CFO shall certify to the board that they have reviewed the financial statements and that they are fair and in compliance with the laws/regulations and accept responsibility for internal control systems.

5. *Report and compliance*

A separate section in the annual report should be on 'compliance with corporate governance'. Also, a quarterly compliance report needs to be submitted to the stock exchange, signed by the compliance officer or CEO.

References

1 'Report of the Committee on the Financial Aspects of Corporate Governance'. 1992. December, www.ecgi.org/codes/documents/cadbury.pdf (accessed on 5 October 2016).
2 OECD. 2004. 'OECD Principles of Corporate Governance', www.oecd.org/corporate/ca/corporategovernanceprinciples/31557724.pdf (accessed on 5 October 2016).
3 SEBI. 2003. 'Report of the Committee on Corporate Governance', 8 February. https://www.sebi.gov.in/reports/reports/mar-2003/the-report-of-shri-n-r-narayana-murthy-committee-on-corporate-governance-for-public-comments-_12986.html
4 OECD. 2016. 'G20/OECD Principles of Corporate Governance', www.oecd.org/ corporate/principles-corporate-governance.htm (accessed on 5 October 2016).
5 OECD Library. 2023. 'G20/OECD Principles of Corporate Governance', https://www.oecd-ilibrary.org/docserver/ed750b30-en.pdf?expires=1696151552&id=id&accname=guest&checksum=FC18A0E0C3AABE920D5CD1A1A4809B4D (accessed on 1 October 2023).

Part IV

Digital finance

8 Fintech

'Fintech' implies the process of integrating technology into financial services or processes for their improvement. Customers now enjoy greater convenience as a result of the financial services' quick digitisation, automation and improvement. Neobanks, *the online-only financial institutions*, allow their clients to order credit cards and open savings accounts online without imposing the same fees as traditional banks. *Peer-to-peer payment apps* and *digital wallets* are examples of other fintech products that have made it simple for consumers to streamline payment procedures. **India is amongst the fastest-growing fintech markets in the world. The Indian fintech industry's Assets Under Management & Revenue is to be $1 trillion and $200 billion by 2030, respectively.**[1]

What is financial technology (Fintech)?

Financial technology (Fintech), a combination of the terms 'financial' and 'technology', *refers to the use of technology to enhance or automate financial services and processes*. The term encompasses a rapidly growing industry that serves the interests of both consumers and businesses in multiple ways. From mobile banking and insurance to cryptocurrency and investment apps, fintech has a seemingly endless array of applications.

Fundamentally, fintech uses specialised software and algorithms that are employed on computers and, increasingly, smartphones to assist organisations, entrepreneurs and individuals in better managing their financial operations, procedures and lives.

DOI: 10.4324/9781003730170-12

The term fintech was first used to describe the technology used in the back-end systems of well-known financial institutions when it first arose in the 21st century. But since then, there has been a shift towards services that are more focused on the needs of the customer and, consequently, a more focused definition. These days, fintech encompasses a wide range of fields and businesses, including investment management, retail banking, education, education and nonprofit fundraising.

Key Characteristics:

- Fintech refers to the integration of technology into offerings by financial services companies in order to improve their use and delivery to consumers.
- It primarily works by unbundling offerings by such firms and creating new markets for them.
- Startups disrupt incumbents in the finance industry by expanding financial inclusion and using technology to cut down on operational costs.

I. Fintech users

There are four broad categories of users for fintech: 1) B2B for banks and 2) their business clients, 3) B2C for small businesses and 4) consumers.

B2B and B2C fintech users and their applications are discussed below:

1. B2B (business to business)

Prior to the development of fintech, companies had to resort to banks for funding and loans. However, the emergence of fintech has made it simple for companies to use mobile technology to obtain loans, funding and other financial services.

In addition, business-to-business (B2B) services like Salesforce (CRM) – Get Free Report and cloud-based platforms enable organisations to engage with financial data to enhance their offerings.

2. *B2C (business to client)*

Fintech, of course, has a lot of business-to-consumer, or B2C, applications. Customers can transfer money using cash applications like PayPal, Venmo and Apple Pay, as well as budgeting apps like Mint, which let users keep track of their spending and finances.

First attempts into fintech by the banking sector were mostly concentrated on B2C applications such as payment services and loans.

Examples of fintech

Fintech has been applied to many areas of finance. Here are a few examples.

- **Roboadvisors** are apps or online platforms that optimally invest your money automatically, often for little cost, and are accessible to the common man.
- **Investment apps** like Robinhood make it easy to buy and sell stocks, ETFs and crypto from your mobile device, often with little or no commission.
- **Payments** apps like Paytm, PayPal and Zelle make it easy to pay individuals or businesses online and in an instant.
- **Personal finance apps** such as Mint, YNAB and Quicken SimpliFi let you see all of your finances in one place, set budgets, pay bills and so on.
- **P2P lending** platforms like Prosper, Lending Club and Upstart allow individuals and small business owners to receive loans from an array of individuals who contribute microloans directly to them.
- **Crypto apps**, including wallets, exchanges and payments applications, allow you to hold and transact in cryptocurrencies and digital tokens like Bitcoin and NFTs.
- **InsurTech** is the application of technology specifically to the insurance space. One example would be the use of devices that monitor your driving in order to adjust auto insurance rates.

The fintech regulation – RBI

Financial services are among the most heavily regulated sectors in the world. Not surprisingly, regulation has emerged as the number one concern among governments as fintech companies take off.

As technology is integrated into financial services processes, regulatory problems for such companies have multiplied. In some instances, the problems are a function of technology. In others, they are a reflection of the tech industry's impatience to disrupt finance. *For instance,* the automation of processes and digitisation of data make fintech systems vulnerable to attacks from hackers. Increasing instances of hacking at credit card companies and banks are illustrations of the ease with which bad actors can gain access to systems and cause irreparable damage. The most important questions for consumers in such cases will pertain to the safety from such attacks, as well as preventing the misuse of personal information and important financial data.

The RBI issued guidelines for **Loans sourced by banks and NBFCs over digital lending platforms** on 24 June 2020,[2] that places responsibilities on the lender to ensure that they adhere to the 'Fair Practice' norms while lending through digital platforms. This is done to guarantee that the final borrower's interests are safeguarded by using the digital platform of another organisation and that he is fully informed about the lending institutions that will finally provide the credit. *For example,* on the websites of banks and NBFCs, the identities of digital lending platforms that are acting as agents must be revealed. Furthermore, the name of the bank or NBFC that the digital lending platforms serving as agents are dealing with directly with the customer must be disclosed. As a result, embedded lending can be considered regulated inasmuch as the financial institutions that extend credit in the end are required to make sure that, while finding clients via digital lending platforms, they comply with the criteria for digital lending.

RBI came up with a framework for NBFC–Account Aggregators (NBFC-AA),[3] which is essentially an entity that pulls financial data of the customer from various sources and aggregates it in a specific manner for use by relevant parties, such as lending institutions. These organisations are essential to the embedded lending model because they extract financial data for banks and NBFCs to use in their credit underwriting procedures and are also a part of the integration with the lending service providers (LSP). Instead of the present 'balance sheet'-based lending model, this aggregation of financial information from the NBFC-AAs and the information already accessible with the LSPs allow the lending activity to become more 'cash flow-based'.

Types of fintech companies'

I. Mobile banking and neobanks

Mobile banking is the central focus of many finance technology companies. In the world of personal finance, consumers wish to have easy access to their bank accounts, especially on a mobile device. Most major banks now offer some kind of mobile banking feature, especially with the rise of digital-first banks, or neobanks. 'Neobanks' are essentially banks without any physical branch locations, serving customers with checking, savings, payment services and loans on a completely mobile and digital infrastructure. Some banks also allow third-party software applications to access a user's financial information, which is called open banking. Some examples of fintech banks or neobanks are *SBI Yono, Paytm, Freo, Mahila Money, Jupiter, etc.*

II. Digital wallets – payment fintech

Digital wallets, like Google Pay, allow people to store their payment information in a mobile app, and then use that app when it comes time to pay for something. While digital wallets have been around for years, their usage is still on the rise.

One thing fintech excels at is money movement. The expression 'I'll pay you later' has been replaced with 'I'll CashApp you'. Naturally, these are the preferred mobile payment methods. The way we all conduct business has been altered by payment businesses. Digital money transfers to any location in the world are now simpler than ever. Popular payment firms include *PhonePe, Paytm, PayPal and Square.*

III. *Cryptocurrency fintech*

Fintech interacts with cryptocurrency and blockchain in a variety of ways. To begin with, a number of cryptocurrency trading platforms have surfaced in recent times, enabling users to trade various cryptocurrency types and benefit from decentralised exchanges.

Additionally, a plethora of cryptocurrency wallets have emerged to safeguard users' digital currency. Blockchain technology is being utilised by a number of fintech businesses for safe digital identity management, money transfers and payment processing. Fintech businesses that deal with cryptocurrencies include *Unocoin, Blockfi and Coinbase.*

IV. *Fintech investment planning*

The number of apps for savings and investment planning has skyrocketed in recent years due to fintech. Businesses like Robinhood, Stash and Acorns are tearing down barriers to investing more than ever. Although these applications take different approaches, they all expose users to the markets by combining automatic small-dollar investing techniques with savings, including fast round-up contributions on purchases.

V. *Machine learning and trading*

For a financier, predicting market direction is the ultimate goal. It should come as no surprise that machine learning has become more and more significant in fintech, particularly in trading, given the billions of dollars that can be made. This AI subset's power in finance comes from its capacity to process vast amounts of data through algorithms made to identify trends and risks. This gives customers, businesses, banks and other organisations a better understanding of the risks associated with investments and purchases early in the process.

VI. *Blockchain in fintech*

Blockchain – a public ledger capable of recording the ownership, origin and movement of digital assets – will continue to impact the financial industry. For beginners, the sector will become much more efficient and secure because to the widespread use of smart contracts and ledger technology.

VII. Fintech lending

Fintech is also revolutionising credit by expediting approval procedures, simplifying risk assessment and facilitating simpler access. Today, mobile devices are used by billions of people worldwide to request loans, and new data points and risk modelling tools are enabling lending to previously underprivileged groups. Furthermore, consumers can obtain credit reports on many occasions a year without experiencing a negative impact on their score, hence increasing transparency throughout the lending industry. Notable businesses in the fintech lending sector are Tala, Petal and Credit Karma.

VIII. Insurtech – insurance fintech

Insurtech is rapidly developing into a separate sector of the economy, and fintech still governs it. Since the insurance industry adopts technology slowly, a lot of fintech firms are collaborating with established insurance providers to increase coverage and automate procedures. The industry is facing a ton of innovation, from wearables for health insurance to mobile auto insurance. Coverfox, Go Digit Insurance, Insurify and Kin are a few insurtech startups to watch.

IX. Embedded finance

Embedded finance (EmFi) is the term for when a non-financial business integrates fintech tools into its point of service. It is a concept that typically allows non-financial entities to integrate financial services/products into their own platform through the use of an API ('Application Programming Interface'), which is a software intermediary that allows two applications to talk to each other. Coffee shop payment terminals and buy-now-pay-later buttons on online store checkouts are two examples.

Take another example, let's say you want to purchase a flight ticket. You reach the payment stage and see an option to purchase insurance as well, without having to leave the app you are currently using. This integration of an insurance purchase on a non-financial entity's platform is just one small part of the bigger picture of embedded finance.

The idea of having everything in one place at high speeds is what drives trade in this modern world. This is where embedded finance would come into play.

Leading fintech companies in India

I. Paytm

One of the first and most well-known mobile payment and financial services companies in India is Paytm, which stands for 'pay through mobile'. The current MD and CEO of the company, Vijay Shekhar Sharma, created it in 2000.

Paytm offers banking, lending, insurance and payment services to both customers and businesses. The company provides online services such as mobile recharges; utility bill payments; bookings for travel, movies and events; as well as in-store payments at grocery stores, restaurants, parking lots, pharmacies and educational institutions using the Paytm QR Code. It also offers loan disbursement services and commerce facilitation for small businesses.

On 18 November 2021, One97 Communications Limited (OCL), its parent firm, went public on Indian stock exchanges after the country's largest-ever IPO at the time.

II. Lendingkart

In order to provide a digital financing platform for SMEs, former banker Harshvardhan Lunia and former ISRO scientist Mukul Sachan created Lendingkart in 2014.

The company determines risk, finds fraud, evaluates consumer creditworthiness and disburses loans in less than 72 hours using machine learning algorithms and big data analytics technologies. For the primary underwriting procedure, data models are created by Lendingkart's own data science and data engineering team.

ML training models are the foundation of the entire loan approval and underwriting process.

Lendingkart was among the first online lenders to use artificial intelligence and machine learning to automate the underwriting process, enabling borrowers with poor credit ratings to be approved for loans.

III. Shiksha Finance

Shiksha Finance lends money to students for their school tuition as well as educational institutions for operating capital, asset creation and infrastructure development. Asset Finance and Study Loans are its two primary offerings.

Its goal is to provide funding to entrepreneurs in the education sector who wish to increase low- and middle-class communities' access to high-quality education.

IV. Pine Labs

Pine Labs was founded in 1998 and initially worked on creating a card-based payment and loyalty system for the retail petroleum sector. Since 2012, they have been reimagining their business plan to adapt to the evolving demands of their merchants. The intelligent, cloud-based, unified point-of-sale (PoS) platform was subsequently invented by it.

In addition to changing the payments and fintech sectors, Pine Labs has aided in the growth of the global digital economy. More than 100,000 merchants in India and other Asian nations use Pine Labs. It is one of the most established Indian firms that invented card-based payment.

V. PolicyBazaar

India's top marketplace and aggregator for insurance products is called PolicyBazaar. When the business was first established in 2008, it compared the costs of insurance policies and offered information about insurance. The organisation assists with policy cancellation and renewal, as well as claim settlement, in addition to acting as an insurance marketplace.

PolicyBazaar facilitates the comparison of financial products and policies for consumers and small enterprises.

Table 8.1 presents fintech unicorns of 2025 worldwide.

Table 8.1 **Fintech unicorns – 2025**

Company	*Valuation ($bn)*	*Country*	*Venture Capital raised ($ mn)*
Revolut	$65	United Kingdom	2,000
Nu Holdings	$41.5	Brazil	1,200
Checkout	$40	United Kingdom	1,800
Robinhood	$32	United States	5,600
Chime	$25	United States	2,600
Citadel Securities	$22	United States	1,100
JD Digits	$19.	China	2,100
Ripple	$15	United States	325
Marqeta	$14.3	United States	525
Plaid	$13.4	United States	734

Source: https://beinsure.com/ranking/biggest-fintech-unicorn-startups-in-world/ (accessed on 9 September 2025).

References

1 Jhunjhunwala, Yogesh. (2023). FDI in FinTech, May 29. https://www.investindia.gov.in/team-india-blogs/fdi-fintech
2 https://www.rbi.org.in/scripts/BS_CircularIndexDisplay.aspx?Id=11920
3 https://www.rbi.org.in/scripts/BS_ViewMasDirections.aspx?id=10598

Part V

Taxation

9 Direct taxation

Income tax

The government receives the majority of its revenue from taxes. This money is used for a variety of national development initiatives and goals. India's tax system is well-developed and always changing, derived from the Indian Constitution. Every tax must have a companion legislation approved by the State Legislature or the Parliament. When compared to the same period last year, India's direct tax collections increased by 15.9% to a record Rs 16.16 lakh crore on March 31, 2023.[1] Due diligence and a thorough understanding of the tax laws and the related rules and regulations are necessary for taxpayers to plan their taxes in a healthy manner. The income tax in India is covered in this chapter. Goods and Services Tax is discussed in the next chapter.

Indian tax structure: overview

The tax structure in India is a three-tier federal structure: the central government, state governments and local municipal bodies. There are two types of taxes – *direct and indirect tax*. Direct taxes are paid by the assessee, while indirect taxes are levied on goods and services. The Indian taxation system has witnessed several modifications over the years. There has been standardisation of income tax rates with simpler governing laws for the understanding of the common man. The net result has been the ease of paying taxes, improved compliance and enhanced enforcement of the laws.

DOI: 10.4324/9781003730170-14

I. *Revenue authority*

These revenue authorities are a part of the Department of Revenue under the Ministry of Finance, Government of India. They are classified as follows:

1. *Central Board of Direct Taxes (CBDT)*

The CBDT provides inputs for policy and planning of direct taxes in India and is responsible for the administration of direct tax laws through the Income Tax Department.

2. *Central Board of Indirect Taxes & Customs (CBIC)*

The CBIC is responsible for the formulation of policy concerning the levy and collection of customs, GST, central excise, service tax and narcotics in India and their administration.

Direct versus indirect tax: distinction

Direct tax is levied directly on individuals and corporate entities and cannot be transferred to others. *Examples of direct tax include* income tax, wealth tax, gift tax and capital gains tax.

Income tax. . .

This is the largest form of direct tax. It is applicable to both individuals and companies. As per the Income Tax Act, 1961, every assessee whose total income exceeds the maximum exempt limit is liable to pay this tax. The tax structure rates and revisions are annually prescribed by the Parliament in the Finance Act, commonly known as the Annual Budget. This tax is imposed during each assessment year, which commences on 1 April and ends on 31 March.

The total income is calculated under one or more of the following heads: *salary, house property, business or profession, capital gain and other sources.*[2]

Indirect taxes are indirectly levied on the public through goods and services. The sellers of the goods and services collect the tax, which is then deposited with the government bodies.

As a significant step towards the reform of indirect taxation in India, the central government had introduced the Goods and Services Tax (GST) on July 1, 2017. GST is a comprehensive indirect tax on the manufacture, sale and consumption of goods and services throughout India and incorporates many indirect taxes levied by the central and state governments.

GST has replaced excise, service tax and various other indirect taxes in India. Now, there are majorly two types of indirect taxes in India – GST and customs.

Basic terminologies under Income Tax Act, 1961

1 **Assessment Year [Sec. 2(9)]:** This is the year in which income is taxable and refers to the period of 12 months starting from April 1 and ending on March 31 of the next year. *For example*, the assessment year of 2022–23 will be 2023–24 and commence on 1 April 2023 and will end on 31 March 2024.

2 **Previous Year [Sec. 3]:** It is the year in which income is earned and means 'the financial year immediately preceding the assessment year'. The income earned in the previous year is taxable in the next year, i.e., the assessment year. So, the income earned during the previous year 2022–23 is taxable in the assessment year 2023–24.

3 **Assessee [Sec. 2(7)]:** This means a person by whom any tax or any other sum of money is payable under the Income Tax Act, 1961.

4 **Person [Sec. 2(31)]:** The term 'person' includes:

   (i) an individual (e.g., Ram, Mohan, Jack);
   (ii) a Hindu undivided family (HUF) (e.g., joint family business of Mr. A, Mrs. A and their sons);
   (iii) a company (e.g., Reliance Industries Ltd., ONGC Ltd.);
   (iv) a firm (e.g., AB and Co., Amit and Associates);
   (v) an association of persons or a body of individuals, whether incorporated or not (e.g., X and Y, the legal heirs of their father, decide to carry on his business);

(vi) a local authority (e.g., North Delhi Municipal Corporation); and
(vii) every artificial juridical person not falling within any of the preceding sub-clauses (e.g., University of Delhi).

5 **Income [Sec. 2(24)]:** The term 'income' includes:

(i) profits and gains;
(ii) dividend;
(iii) voluntary contributions received by a trust created wholly or partly for charitable or religious purposes or by an institution established wholly or partly for such purposes or by an association or institution, or by a fund or trust or institution or by any university or other educational institution or by any hospital or other institution or by an electoral trust;
(iv) the value of any perquisite or profit in lieu of salary;
(v) any special allowance or benefit, specifically granted to the assessee to meet expenses wholly, necessarily and exclusively for the performance of his duties;
(vi) any allowance granted to the assessee either to meet his personal expenses at the place where he performs his duties or to compensate him for the increased cost of living;
(vii) the value of any benefit or perquisite, whether convertible into money or not, obtained from a company either by a director or by a person who has a substantial interest in the company, or by a relative of the director or such person;
(viii) the value of any benefit or perquisite, whether convertible into money or not, obtained by any representative assessee or beneficiary and any sum paid by the representative assessee in respect of any obligation which, but for such payment, would have been payable by the beneficiary;
(ix) any sum chargeable to income tax under clauses (ii), (iii), (iiia), (iiib), (iiic), (iv) and (v) of section 28 or clauses (ii) and (iii) of section 41 or section 59;
(x) any capital gains;

(xi) the profits and gains of any business of insurance carried on by a mutual insurance company or by a cooperative society;

(xii) the profits and gains of any business of banking carried on by a cooperative society;

(xiii) any winnings from lotteries, crossword puzzles, races, including horse races, card games and other games of any sort or from gambling or betting of any form or nature whatsoever;

(xiv) any sum received by the assessee from his employees as contributions to any provident fund or superannuation fund or any fund set up under the provisions of the Employees' State Insurance Act 1948 (34 of 1948), or any other fund for the welfare of such employees;

(xv) any sum received under a Keyman insurance policy, including the sum allocated by way of bonus on such policy;

(xvi) any sum referred to in clause *(va)* of section 28;

(xvii) the fair market value of inventory referred to in clause (*via*) of section 28;

(xviii) any sum referred to in clause (*v*) and *(vi)* of sub-section (2) of section 56;

(xix) any sum of money or value of property referred to in clause (*vii*) or clause (*viia*) of sub-section (2) of section 56;

(xx) any consideration received for the issue of shares that exceeds the fair market value of the shares referred to in clause (*viib*) of sub-section (2) of section 56;

(xxi) any sum of money referred to in clause (*ix*) of sub-section (2) of section 56;

(xxii) any sum of money or value of property referred to in clause (*x*) of sub-section (2) of section 56;

(xxiii) any compensation or other payment referred to in clause (*xi*) of sub-section (2) of section 56;

(xxiv) assistance in the form of a subsidy or grant or cash incentive or duty drawback or waiver or concession or reimbursement (by whatever name called) by the central government or a State Government or any authority or body or agency in cash or kind to the assessee.[3]

PAN & TAN

PAN (permanent account number) is a ten-digit unique alphanumeric number issued by the Income Tax Department in the form of a laminated plastic card. It enables the department to identify/link all transactions of the PAN holder with the department. Every assessee has to obtain a PAN.

TAN or tax deduction and collection account number is a 10-digit alphanumeric number required to be obtained by all persons who are responsible for deducting or collecting tax. Under Section 203A of the Income Tax Act, 1961, it is mandatory to quote TAN allotted by the Income Tax Department on all TDS returns.

6 **Residence in India [Sec. 6]:** The related provisions are as follows:

(1) An individual is said to be resident in India in any previous year, if he:

  (i) is in India in that year for a period or periods amounting in all to 182 days or more; or
  (ii) having within the four years preceding that year been in India for a period or periods amounting in all to 365 days or more, is in India for a period or periods amounting in all to 60 days or more in that year.

(2) A Hindu undivided family, firm or other association of persons is said to be resident in India in any previous year in every case except where during that year the control and management of its affairs is situated wholly outside India.

(3) A company is said to be a resident in India in any previous year, if:

  (i) it is an Indian company; or
  (ii) its place of effective management, in that year, is in India.

(4) Every other person is said to be resident in India in any previous year in every case, except where during that year the control and management of his affairs is situated wholly outside India.

(5) If a person is resident in India in a previous year relevant to an assessment year in respect of any source of income, he shall be deemed to be resident in India in the previous year relevant to the assessment year in respect of each of his other sources of income.

A person is said to be 'not ordinarily resident' in India in any previous year if such person is:

(a) an individual who has been a non-resident in India in nine out of the ten previous years preceding that year, or has during the seven previous years preceding that year been in India for a period of, or periods amounting in all to, 729 days or less;
or

(b) a Hindu undivided family whose manager has been a non-resident in India in nine out of the ten previous years preceding that year, or has during the seven previous years preceding that year been in India for a period of, or periods amounting in all to, 729 days or less.

(c) a citizen of India, or a person of Indian origin, having total income, other than the income from foreign sources, exceeding 15 lakh rupees during the previous year, who has been in India for a period or periods amounting in all to 120 days or more but less than 182 days; or

(d) a citizen of India who is deemed to be resident in India under clause (*1A*). [4]

Income tax classification

According to Section 14 of the Income Tax Act, 1961, for the purposes of charge of income tax and computation of total income, all income is classified under the following heads of income:

A. Salaries
B. Income from house property
C. Profits and gains of business or profession
D. Capital gains
E. Income from other sources

I. Salaries [Sec. 15]

The following income shall be chargeable to income tax under the head 'Salaries':

(a) any salary due from an employer or a former employer to an assessee in the previous year, whether paid or not;
(b) any salary paid or allowed to him in the previous year by or on behalf of an employer or a former employer, though not due or before it became due to him;
(c) any arrears of salary paid or allowed to him in the previous year by or on behalf of an employer or a former employer, if not charged to income tax for any earlier previous year.[5]

Salary [Sec. 17] includes:

(i) wages;
(ii) any annuity or pension;
(iii) any gratuity;
(iv) any fees, commissions, perquisites or profits in lieu of or in addition to any salary or wages;
(v) any advance of salary;
(vi) any payment received by an employee in respect of any period of leave not availed of by him;
(vii) the annual accretion to the balance at the credit of an employee participating in a recognised provident fund;

(viii) the aggregate of all sums that are comprised in the transferred balance of an employee participating in a recognised provident fund; and

(ix) the contribution made by the central government or any other employer in the previous year, to the account of an employee under a pension scheme referred to in section 80CCD.

(x) [*the contribution made by the central government in the previous year, to the* Agniveer *Corpus Fund account of an individual enrolled in the* Agnipath *Scheme referred to in section 80CCH.*][6]

II. Income from house property [Sec. 22]

The annual value of property consisting of any buildings or lands of which the assessee is the owner, not occupied for the purposes of any business or profession carried on by him, the profits of which are chargeable to income tax, shall be chargeable to income tax under the head 'Income from house property'.[7]

III. Profits and gains of business or profession [Sec. 28]

The following income shall be chargeable to income tax under the head 'Profits and gains of business or profession':

(i) the profits and gains of any business or profession that was carried on by the assessee at any time during the previous year;

(ii) any compensation or other payment due to or received by:

  (a) any person, managing the whole or substantially the whole of the affairs of an Indian company;

  (b) any person, managing the whole or substantially the whole of the affairs in India of any other company;

  (c) any person, holding an agency in India for any part of the activities relating to the business of any other person;

(d) any person, for or in connection with the vesting in the government, or in any corporation owned or controlled by the government, under any law for the time being in force, of the management of any property or business;
(e) any person, by whatever name called, at or in connection with the termination or the modification of the terms and conditions of any contract relating to his business;
(f) others.[8]

IV. Capital gains [Sec. 45]

Any profits or gains arising from the transfer of a capital asset effected in the previous year shall, save as otherwise provided in sections 54, 54B, 54D, 54E, 54EA, 54EB, 54F, 54G and 54H, be chargeable to income tax under the head 'Capital gains', and shall be deemed to be the income of the previous year in which the transfer took place.[9]

Income from capital gains is classified as 'Short-term capital gains' and 'Long-term capital gains'.

(a) *Short-term capital asset.* Any capital asset held by the tax-payer for a period of not more than 36 months immediately preceding the date of its transfer will be treated as a short-term capital asset.
(b) *Long-term capital asset.* Any capital asset held by the tax-payer for a period of more than 36 months immediately preceding the date of its transfer will be treated as a long-term capital asset.

However, in respect of certain assets like shares (equity or preference) that are listed in a recognised stock exchange in India, units of equity-oriented mutual funds, listed securities like debentures and government securities, units of UTI and Zero-coupon Bonds, the period of holding to be considered is 12 months instead of 36 months.[10]

V. Income from other sources [Sec. 56]

Income of every kind under the Act shall be chargeable to income tax under the head 'Income from other sources', if it is not chargeable to income tax under any of the heads specified in Section 14, items A to E.

In particular, the following incomes shall be chargeable to income tax under the head 'Income from other sources', namely:

(i) dividends;
(ii) income referred to in sub-clause (viii), (ix), (x) and (xi) of clause (24) of Section 2;
(iii) income by way of interest on securities;
(iv) income from machinery, plant or furniture belonging to the assessee and let on hire;
(v) where an assessee lets on hire machinery, plant or furniture belonging to him and also buildings, and the letting of the buildings is inseparable from the letting of the said machinery, plant or furniture, the income from such letting;
(vi) where any sum of money exceeding Rs. 25,000 is received without consideration by an individual or a Hindu undivided family from any person on or after 1 September 2004 but before 1 April 2006, the whole of such sum;
(vii) where any sum of money, the aggregate value of which exceeds Rs. 50,000, is received without consideration, by an individual or a Hindu undivided family, in any previous year from any person or persons on or after 1 April 2006 but before 1 October 2009, the whole of the aggregate value of such sum;
(viii) where an individual or a Hindu undivided family receives, in any previous year, from any person or persons on or after 1 October 2009 [but before 1 April 2017]:

  (a) any sum of money, without consideration, exceeding Rs. 50,000,
  (b) any immovable property,
  (c) any property, other than immovable property.

(ix) where a firm or a company not being a company in which the public are substantially interested, receives, in any previous year, from any person or persons, on or after 1 June 2010 [but before 1 April 2017], any property, being shares of a company not being a company in which the public are substantially interested;
(x) where a company, not being a company in which the public are substantially interested, receives, in any previous year, from any person being a resident, any consideration for the

issue of shares that exceeds the face value of such shares, the aggregate consideration received for such shares as exceeds the fair market value of the shares;

(xi) income by way of interest received on compensation or on enhanced compensation referred to in clause (b) of Section 145A;

(xii) any sum of money received as an advance or otherwise in the course of negotiations for the transfer of a capital asset;

(xiii) others.[11]

Computation of tax liability

After ascertaining the total income for the year, as discussed earlier, the tax liability of the taxpayer is computed. Table 9.1 provides an overview of the computation of tax liability for the year.

I. Individual Tax

For individuals, the tax to be paid by them depends on the tax bracket they fall in. This bracket or slab determines the tax to be paid based on the annual income of the assessee and ranges from zero tax to 30% tax for the high-income groups.

The government fixes different tax slabs for various groups of individuals under the Finance Act every year: general taxpayers, senior citizens (people aged between 60 and 80) and super senior citizens (people aged over 80).

Gross total income versus total income

Gross total income (GTI) is the sum of your (i) income from salary,

(ii) income from house property, (iii) profits or gains from business or profession, (iv) capital gains and (v) income from other sources. It is the total amount of money you have earned from all your sources of income

Total income or taxable income is basically your GTI minus deductions under Section 80C to Section 80U.

Table 9.1 Computation of tax liability on total income of an INDIVIDUAL for the year

Particulars	*Amount*
Income from salary	XXXXX
Income from house property	XXXXX
Profits and gains of business or profession	XXXXX
Capital gains	XXXXX
Income from other sources	XXXXX
Gross total income	***XXXXX***
Less: Deductions under Chapter VI-A (i.e., under Section 80C to 80U)	(XXXXX)
Total income (i.e., taxable income)	***XXXXX***
Tax on total income to be computed at the applicable rates	XXXXX
Less: Rebate under Section 87A	(XXXXX)
Tax liability after rebate	***XXXXX***
Add: Surcharge	XXXXX
Tax liability after surcharge	***XXXXX***
Add: Health and Education Cess @ 4% on tax liability after surcharge	XXXXX
Tax liability before rebate under Sections 86, Section 89, Sections 90, 90A and 91 (if any) (*)	XXXXX
Less: Rebate under Sections 86, Section 89, Sections 90, 90A and 91 (if any) (*)	(XXXXX)
Tax liability for the year before prepaid taxes	XXXXX
Less: Prepaid taxes in the form of TDS, TCS and advance tax	(XXXXX)
Tax payable/refundable	***XXXXX***

Source: https://incometaxindia.gov.in/tutorials/79.computation-of-tax-for-individual.pdf (accessed on 4 October 2023).

(*) *Rebate under Section 86:* It is available to a member of association of persons (AOP) or body of individuals (BOI) in respect of income received by such member from the AOP/BOI.

Rebate under Section 87A: The rebate is available to a resident individual if his total income does not exceed Rs. 5,00,000. The amount of rebate shall be 100% of income tax or Rs. 12,500, whichever is less.

Rebate (i.e., relief) under section 89: It is available to a salaried employee in respect of sum received towards arrears of salary, gratuity, etc.

Rebate under sections 90, 90A and 91: It is available to a taxpayer in respect of double-taxed income, i.e., income that is taxed in India as well as abroad.

Notes:

1. One can avail of the deductions only under the 'old tax regime'.
2. However, where an individual opts for the New Tax Regime, the tax on normal income shall be charged at the rates provided under the said section.

Table 9.2 Tax rates for individual(s) for assessment year 2023–24 [**Old tax regime**] *(In case of an Individual (resident or non-resident) or HUF or Association of Person or Body of Individual or any other artificial juridical person)*

Taxable income (Rs.)	*Tax rate 'Individual' [Less than 60 years]*	*Tax rate 'Senior citizen' [60 years – less than 80 years]*	*Tax rate 'Super Senior citizen' [80 years or more]*
Up to Rs. 2,50,000	Nil	Nil	Nil
Rs. 2,50,001 to Rs. 3,00,000	5%	Nil	Nil
Rs. 3,00,001 to Rs. 5,00,000	5%	5%	Nil
Rs. 5,00,001 to Rs. 10,00,000	20%	20%	20%
Above Rs. 10,00,000	30%	30%	30%

Less: Rebate under Section 87A

[explained in Table 9.1 notes]

Add: Surcharge & Health and Education Cess (see note after Table 9.3)

The tax rates for assessment year 2023–24 as per the **Old Income Tax Regime** and for 2024–25 under **New Tax Regime** are given in Tables 9.2 and 9.3.

New tax regime versus old tax regime

A new tax regime was introduced in Budget 2020 wherein the tax slabs were altered, and taxpayers were offered concessional tax rates.

However, those who opt for the new regime cannot claim several exemptions and deductions, such as HRA, LTA, 80C, 80D and more.

Under the older tax regime, there are multiple exemptions and deductions available, including HRA and LTA, that can reduce your taxable income and lower tax payments.

Tax rates in the new regime are the **same for all categories, viz.**

Individuals, Senior citizens and Super senior citizens. The taxpayer opting for concessional rates in this regime will have to forgo these exemptions and deductions available in the existing old tax regime.

Table 9.3 Tax rates for individual(s) for assessment year 2024–25 [**New tax regime**]

Taxable income (Rs.)	*Tax rate*
Up to Rs. 3,00,000	Nil
Rs. 3,00,001 to Rs. 6,00,000	5%
Rs. 6,00,001 to Rs. 9,00,000	10%
Rs. 9,00,001 to Rs. 12,00,000	15%
Rs. 12,00,001 to Rs. 15,00,000	20%
Above Rs. 15,00,000	30%

Add: Surcharge & Health and Education Cess (see note after Table 9.3)

Source: https://incometaxindia.gov.in/tutorials/79.computation-of-tax-for-individual.pdf (accessed on 4 October 2023)

Notes:

(a) New tax regime:

Section 115BAC provides a new tax regime for individuals, which has reduced tax slabs.

However, to avail of the benefit of this tax regime, the assessee has to forgo specified

exemptions and deductions.

(b) Surcharge:

(i) at the rate of 10% of such tax, where total income exceeds Rs. 50 lakhs but does not exceed Rs. 1 crore.

(ii) at the rate of 15% of such tax, where total income exceeds Rs. 1 crore.

(c) Health and Education Cess: at the rate of 4% of such income tax and surcharge.

Illustration 9.1: Mr. Amit is 40 years old and employed in ABC Ltd. The details of his income and investment during financial year 2022–23 are as follows:

Basic pay	Rs. 5,00,000
Incentives	Rs. 1,00,000
House rent allowance	Rs. 1,50,000
Contribution by Amit to Provident Fund	Rs. 36,000
Amount deposited in PPF account	Rs. 50,000
House rent paid for residence in Delhi	Rs. 84,000
LIC premium paid	Rs. 14,000
Medical insurance premium paid	Rs. 20,000
Interest received from savings bank account	Rs. 10,000

Calculate income tax liability as per old tax regime of Amit for assessment year 2023–2024.

Solution

Computation of taxable income

Income from salary:			
Basic Pay		Rs. 5,00,000	
Incentives		Rs. 1,00,000	
House Rent Allowance	Rs. 1,50,000		
Less: Exemption (see note 1)	Rs. 44,000	Rs. 1,06,000	Rs. 7,06,000
Income from other sources:			
Interest received from savings bank account	Rs. 10,000		
Gross Total Income	**Rs. 7,16,000**		
Less: **Deduction under Chapter VI-A Under Section 80C**			
Contribution to Provident Fund	Rs. 36,000	Deposit in PPF Account	Rs. 50,000
LIC Premium paid	Rs. 14,000		Rs. 1,00,000
Medical Insurance Premium Paid			Rs.20,000
Under Section 80TTA			
Interest from savings bank account	Rs. 10,000		Rs. 1,30,000
Taxable Income			**Rs. 5,86,000**
Income tax payable on Rs. 5,86,000/=			Rs. 29,700
Add: Health and Education Cess @ 4%			Rs. 1,188
Total Tax Liability			**Rs. 30,888**

Notes:

1 The amount of HRA exemption is the least of the following:
(i) Actual HRA received Rs. 1,50,000
(ii) Rent paid – 10% of salary, i.e. (84,000 – 40,000) Rs. 44,000
(iii) 50% of salary Rs. 2,00,000
2 Medical Insurance Premium is allowed up to Rs. 25000 as deduction under Section 80D.
3 Deduction under Section 80TTA is allowed up to Rs. 10,000 in respect of interest received from savings bank accounts.
4 A rebate of income tax is not allowed under Section 87A since the taxable income in the above case is more than Rs. 5,00,000. [The amount of rebate is actual income tax payable or Rs. 12,500, whichever is less if the taxable income is up to Rs. 5,00,000.]

II. Cooperative society tax

A cooperative society is taxed as per the slabs. For the assessment years 2023–24 and 2024–25, its taxation is given in Table 9.4.

III. Partnership firm tax

The partnership firm is taxed at flat rate. For the assessment years 2023–24 and 2024–25, a partnership firm (including LLP) is taxable at 30%.

Table 9.4 Tax rates for cooperative society for assessment years 2023–25

Taxable income	*Tax rate*
Up to Rs. 10,000	10%
Rs. 10,000 to Rs. 20,000	20%
Above Rs. 20,000	30%

Source: https://incometaxindia.gov.in/charts%20%20tables/tax%20rates.htm (accessed on 5 October 2023).

Add Surcharge: at the rate of 7% of such tax, where total income exceeds one crore rupees but not exceeding ten crore rupees, and at the rate of 12% of such tax, where total income exceeds ten crore rupees.

Health and Education Cess: The amount of income tax and the applicable surcharge shall be further increased by health and education cess calculated at the rate of 4% of such income tax and surcharge.

Add:

(a) *Surcharge:* at the rate of 12% of such tax, where total income exceeds Rs. 1 crore.
(b) *Health and Education Cess:* at the rate of 4% of such income tax and surcharge.[12]

IV. Local authority tax

The local authority's taxation is also at a flat rate. For the assessment years 2023–24 & 2024–25, a local authority is taxable at 30%.

Add:

(a) *Surcharge:* at the rate of 12% of such tax, where total income exceeds Rs. 1 crore.
(b) *Health and Education Cess:* at the rate of 4% of such income tax and surcharge.[12]

V. Corporate tax

Corporate tax is the income tax that is paid by companies from the revenue they earn. The imposition of such a tax varies from a domestic company to a foreign organisation. For the assessment year 2023–24, the following are the rates of corporate tax, which are levied on different companies:

1. Domestic company

Domestic companies are taxable at 30%. However, the tax rate would be 25% where the total turnover or gross receipts of the company does not exceed Rs. 400 crores during the previous year 2020–21.

[Tax rate (25% or 30%) for assessment year 2024–25 will be determined based on the turnover for the previous year 2021–22.]

Add:

(a) *Surcharge:* at the rate of 7% of such tax, where total income exceeds Rs. 1 crore but not exceeding Rs. 10 crores and at the rate of 12% of such tax, where total income exceeds Rs. 10 crores.

(b) *Health and Education Cess:* at the rate of 4% of such income tax and surcharge.

Minimum alternate tax and AMT

MAT stands for 'minimum alternate tax' and AMT stands for 'alternate minimum tax'. MAT is the minimum tax to be paid by companies, which currently stands at 15%.

Initially, the concept of MAT was introduced for companies, and progressively it has been made applicable to all other taxpayers in the form of AMT.

Objective of MAT

It is possible that a taxpayer, being a company, may have earned income during the year, but by taking advantage of various provisions of income tax law (such as exemptions, deductions, depreciation, etc.), it may have reduced its tax liability or may not have even paid any tax. Due to an increase in the number of zero-taxpaying companies, MAT was introduced by the Finance Act, 1987, with effect from the assessment year 1988–89. Later on, it was withdrawn by the Finance Act, 1990, and then reintroduced by the Finance (No. 2) Act, 1996.

The 'objective' of the introduction of MAT is to bring into the tax net 'zero tax companies', which, in spite of having earned substantial book profits and having paid handsome dividends, do not pay any tax due to various tax concessions and incentives provided under the Income Tax Act.

Basic provisions of MAT

After several changes in MAT, today it is levied on companies as per the provisions of Section 115JB. As per the concept of MAT, the tax liability of a company will be the higher of the following:

- Tax liability of the company computed as per the normal provisions of the Income Tax Act, i.e., tax liability by applying the tax rate applicable to the company. Tax computed in the above manner can be termed as normal tax liability.
- Tax computed @ 15% (plus surcharge and cess as applicable) on book profit (book profit means net profit as shown in the statement of profit and loss prepared in accordance with Schedule III to the Companies Act, 2013) is MAT.

Thus, MAT applies to companies and AMT applies to a person other than a company. In case of a non-corporate taxpayer, AMT is levied @ 18.5% of adjusted total income. Surcharge and cess, as applicable, will also be levied.[13]

Illustration *9.2:* The taxable income of MG Metals Pvt. Ltd., computed as per the provisions of the Income Tax Act for 2022–23, is Rs. 8,40,000. Book profit of the company computed as per the provisions of Section 115JB is Rs. 18,40,000.

What will be the tax liability of the company for the year (ignore cess and surcharge)?

Solution

The tax liability of a company will be the higher of: (i) normal tax liability, or (ii) MAT.

Normal tax rate applicable to an Indian company is 30%* (plus cess and surcharge as applicable).

Tax @ 30% on Rs. 8,40,000 = Rs. 2,52,000 (plus cess). Book profit of the company is Rs. 18,40,000.

MAT liability (excluding cess and surcharge) @ 15% on Rs. 18,40,000

= Rs. 2,76,000.

Thus, the tax liability of MG Metals Pvt. Ltd. = Rs. 2,76,000 *(plus cess as applicable) being higher than the normal tax liability.*

2. *Foreign company*

The nature of income and tax rates for foreign companies for the assessment years 2023–25 is given below.

Nature of income	*Tax rate*
Royalty received from the government or an Indian concern in pursuance of an agreement made with the Indian concern after 31 March 1961, but before 1 April 1976, or fees for rendering technical services in pursuance of an agreement made after 29 February 1964, but before 1 April 1976, and where such agreement has, in either case, been approved by the central government	50%
Any other income	40%

Add:

(a) *Surcharge:* at the rate of 2% of such tax, where total income exceeds Rs. 1 crore but not exceeding Rs. 10 crores and at the rate of 5% of such tax, where total income exceeds Rs. 10 crores.

(b) *Health and Education Cess:* at the rate of 4% of such income tax and surcharge.[12]

References

1 Zee Business, April 3, 2023, https://www.zeebiz.com/personal-finance/income-tax/news-indias-direct-tax-collection-grows-16-to-record-rs-162-lakh-crore-in-2022–23-sources-228809 (accessed on 1 October 2023).

2 Tax Structure and Taxation System in India, www.hdfclife.com/insurance- knowledge-centre/tax-saving-insurance/Tax-Structure-in-India (accessed on 20 August 2018).

3 Section 2, Income Tax Act, 1961–2023, https://incometaxindia.gov.in/Pages/section-wise-statutes.aspx https://indiankanoon.org/doc/789969 (accessed on 24 April 2024).
4 Section 6, Income Tax Act, 1961–2023, https://incometaxindia.gov.in/Pages/section-wise-statutes.aspx (accessed on 4 October 2023).
5 Section 15, Income Tax Act, 1961–2023, https://incometaxindia.gov.in/Pages/section-wise-statutes.aspx (accessed on 4 October 2023).
6 Section 17, Income Tax Act, 1961–2023, https://incometaxindia.gov.in/Pages/section-wise-statutes.aspx (accessed on 4 October 2023).
7 Section 22, Income Tax Act, 1961–2023, https://incometaxindia.gov.in/Pages/section-wise-statutes.aspx (accessed on 4 October 2023).
8 Section 28, Income Tax Act, 1961–2023, https://incometaxindia.gov.in/Pages/section-wise-statutes.aspx (accessed on 4 October 2023).
9 Section 45, Income Tax Act, 1961–2023, https://incometaxindia.gov.in/Pages/section-wise-statutes.aspx (accessed on 4 October 2023).
10 Tax on Long-Term Capital Gains, https://incometaxindia.gov.in/tutorials/15-%20ltcg.pdf (accessed on 4 October 2023).
11 Section 56, Income Tax Act, 1961–2023, https://incometaxindia.gov.in/Pages/section-wise-statutes.aspx (accessed on 4 October 2023).
12 Tax Rates, https://incometaxindia.gov.in/charts%20%20tables/tax%20rates.htm (accessed on 5 October 2023).
13 MAT and AMT, https://incometaxindia.gov.in/tutorials/10.mat-and-amt.pdf (accessed on 5 October 2023).

10 Indirect taxation

Goods and Services Tax

Indirect taxes form a sizeable portion of the government income. These taxes are levied by adding them to the price of the product or service, which increases their cost. As an indirect tax, Goods and Services Tax (GST) has brought in a 'one nation, one tax' system, and is structured for efficient tax collection, reduction in corruption, easy inter-state movement of goods and many more. It applies to all types of businesses, small or large. This has been a new chapter in the process of tax reforms in the country. Gross GST collections reached a record high of Rs 22.08 lakh crore in the 2024–25 fiscal year, showing a remarkable increase from Rs 11.37 lakh crore in FY21, effectively doubling in five years.[1]

Concept of Goods and Services Tax

Goods and Services Tax (GST) is an 'indirect tax' that has replaced many central and state indirect taxes (like central sales tax, excise duty, service tax, and value-added tax) levied on goods and services in India. The Goods and Services Tax Act was passed in the Parliament on 29 March 2017. The Act came into effect on 1 July 2017. Goods and Services Tax law in India is a comprehensive, multi-stage and destination-based tax that is levied on every value addition. It is considered to be the biggest tax reform in the Indian tax structure, which is oriented to simplify the old taxation system.

> In simple words, GST is 'one indirect tax for the entire country'. It means tax on the supply of goods and services.

DOI: 10.4324/9781003730170-15

VAT (value-added tax)* and GST are sometimes used interchangeably, as the latter denotes comprehensiveness of VAT by coverage of goods and services. France was the first country to implement

* VAT is a consumption tax levied on a product whenever value is added at each stage of the supply chain, from production to the point of sale.

VAT in 1954. Presently, more than 160 countries have implemented GST/VAT in some form or the other. The most popular form of VAT is where taxes paid on inputs are allowed to be adjusted in the liability at the output. The VAT or GST regimes in practice varies from one country to another in terms of their technical aspects such as 'definition of supply', 'extent of coverage of goods and services', 'treatment of exemptions and zero rating', etc. However, at a broader level, they have one common principle, each is a 'destination-based consumption tax'.[2]

Application of GST

I. Key features of GST

1. Dual system

GST is applicable on both goods and services and India follows a 'dual system' of GST to keep both the centre and the state independent of each other.

There are two types of GST structures in the world. These are:

(i) Single GST
(ii) Dual GST

India has adopted the dual GST system, like Canada, wherein both the centre and states administer tax independently. In this, central GST and state GST are levied on the taxable value of every transaction of supply of goods and services. The threshold limit for exemption is Rs. 20 lakhs (and Rs. 40 lakhs for a supplier of goods (Intra-state) in India). The new system, called 'GST 2.0', simplifies taxes into a two-slab structure. The government currently has two tax slab rates: 5% and 18% for various items, with some goods and services exempted, as presented in Figure 10.1.

There are Super luxury and Sin goods, such as luxury cars, and tobacco and tobacco-related products, for example, cigarettes, pan masala, which have been slapped with a 40 per cent levy.

2. *Comprehensive in nature*

GST is one tax that replaces the following indirect taxes that were previously levied by the centre and the state. Figure 10.1 presents GST rate slabs:

(i) Taxes levied and collected by the centre:

1 Central excise duty
2 Excise duty levied under Medicinal & Toilet Preparation Act
3 Additional duties of excise
4 Additional and special additional duties of customs
5 Service tax
6 Central Surcharges and cesses

(ii) Taxes levied and collected by the state:

1 State VAT
2 Central sales tax
3 Luxury tax
4 Entry tax
5 Entertainment and amusement tax
6 Taxes on advertisements
7 Purchase tax
8 Taxes on lottery, betting and gambling
9 State Surcharges and cesses

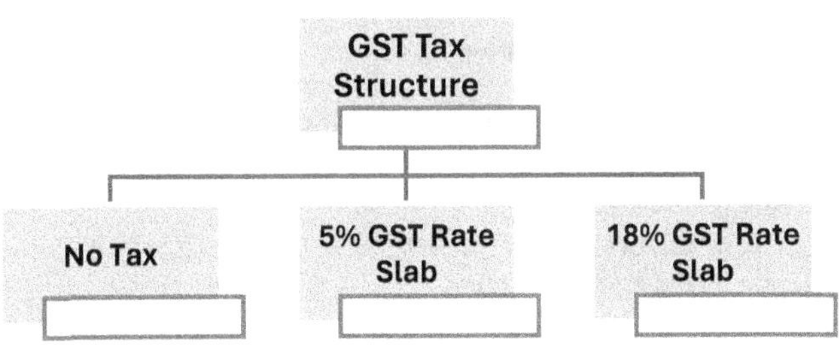

Figure 10.1 GST rate slabs.

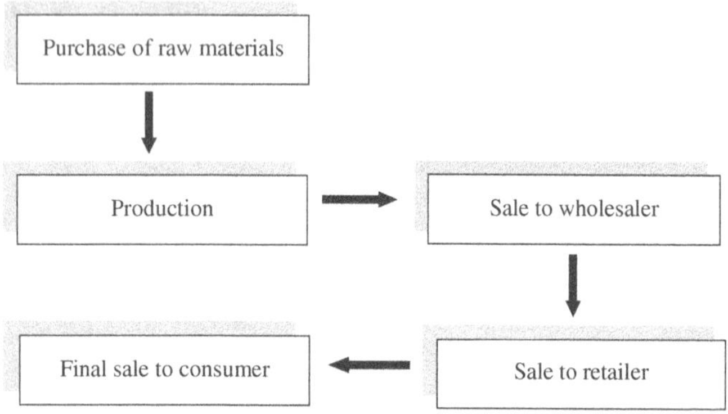

Figure 10.2 Supply chain of GST.

Figure 10.2 above depicts the GST supply chain.

1. *Multi-stage*

Under the GST regime, the tax will be levied at every point of sale, that is, on each stage of the value chain, from the procurement of raw material to the sale of the finished product to the end-consumer, whenever there is value addition and transfer of ownership.

In case of *intra-state sales,* the Central Goods and Services Tax (CGST) and the State Goods and Services Tax (SGST) will be charged. *Inter-state sales* will be chargeable to Integrated GST.

There are multiple change-of-hands that an item goes through along its supply chain: from manufacture to final sale to the consumer.

Let us consider the following chain:

- Purchase of raw materials
- Production or manufacture
- Sale to wholesaler
- Sale of the product to retailer
- Sale to the end-consumer

Goods and Services Tax is levied on each of these stages, which makes it a 'multi-stage tax'.

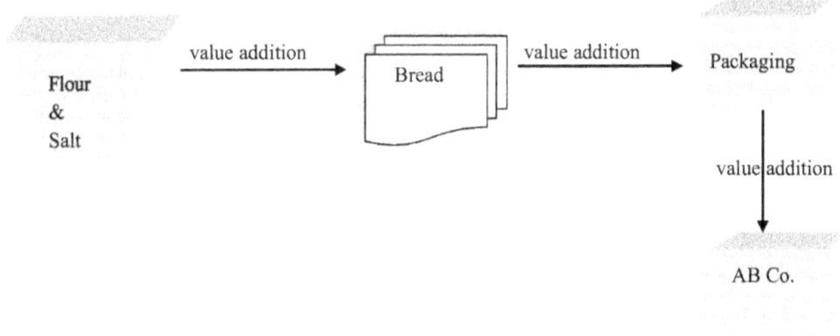

Figure 10.3 Value addition in GST.

2. *Value addition*

GST is levied on the supply of goods and services at every stage of value addition. This is presented in Figure 10.3.

The example in Figure 10.3 is explained as follows:

1 The manufacturer who makes bread buys flour, salt and other materials. The value of the inputs increases when the salt and flour are mixed and baked into bread.
2 The manufacturer then sells the bread to the packaging agent, who packs large quantities of bread. That is another addition of value, after which it is sold to the retailer.
3 The retailer packages the bread in smaller quantities and labels it as 'AB Co. Bread' after due marketing, thus increasing its value.

GST will be levied on these value additions, that is, the monetary worth added at each stage to achieve the final sale to the end customer.

3. *Destination-based*

GST is destination-based because the final purchase is the place where the government collects GST. ***Considering the above example,*** bread is manufactured in Delhi and is sold to the final consumer in Uttar Pradesh. Since GST is levied at the point of consumption, in this case, the entire tax revenue will go to Uttar Pradesh and not Delhi.

4. *Compensation to states*

The Goods and Services Tax (Compensation to States) Act, 2017, provides for compensation to the states for the loss of revenue arising on account of the implementation of the GST. The compensation will be provided to a state for a period of five years from the date on which the state brings its SGST Act into force. For the purpose of calculating the compensation amount payable in any financial year, the year 2015–16 will be taken as the base year for calculating the revenue to be protected.[2]

5. *Anti-profiteering mechanism*

Implementation of GST in many countries was coupled with an increase in inflation and the prices of commodities. This happened in spite of the availability of the tax credit. This happened because the supplier was not passing on the benefit to the consumer and thereby indulging in illegal profiteering. Any reduction in the rate of tax or the benefit of increased 'input tax credit' should be passed on to the recipient by way of commensurate reduction in prices.

The National Anti-Profiteering Authority (NAPA) has been constituted under GST by the central government to examine the complaints of non-passing the benefit of reduced tax incidence.[2]

GST and cascading effect

In the pre-GST regime, every buyer, including the end-consumer, paid tax on tax. This tax on tax is called the 'cascading effect of taxes'. GST avoids this cascading effect as the tax is calculated only on the value added at each stage of transfer of ownership.

Taking the ***above example of Figure 10.3 further and assigning numbers,*** the 'tax computation' pre- and post-GST is explained below.

Tax calculation earlier [pre-GST]:

Transaction	*Cost*	*10% tax (VAT)*	*Total*
Manufacturer	1,000	100	1,100
Packaging agent repacks @ 200	1,300	130	1,430
Retailer advertises and labels @ 400	1,830	183	2,013
Total	**1,600**	**413**	**2,013**

It can be seen that earlier the tax liability was passed on at every stage of the transaction, and the final liability comes on the customer. This is called the 'cascading effect of taxes', where a tax is paid on tax and the value of the item keeps increasing every time.

Tax calculation under GST [post-GST]:

Transaction	*Cost*	*10% tax*	*Actual liability*	*Total*
Manufacturer	1,000	100	100	1,100
Packaging agent repacks @ 200	1,200	120	20	1,320
Retailer advertises and labels @ 400	1,600	160	40	1,760
Total	**1,600**		**160**	**1,760**

In the case of GST, someone can claim credit for tax paid in acquiring input when they submit their taxes.

In the end, every time an individual claims 'input tax credit', the sale price is reduced, and ultimately the cost price for the buyer is reduced because of a lower tax liability. The final value of the bread is therefore reduced from Rs. 2,013 to Rs. 1,760, thus reducing the tax burden on the final customer.

GST mechanism

There are three taxes applicable under this system: CGST, SGST and IGST.

- **CGST (Central Goods and Services Tax)** is collected by the central government on an intra-state sale of goods and services. It is levied alongside SGST or UGST, and the collected revenues are shared equally between the centre and the state.
  For example, a business in Maharashtra supplies 1 tonne of iron ore to a consumer within the state. The GST then diverts to the central government and the 'Maharashtra government'.
- **SGST (State Goods and Services Tax)** is collected by the state government on an intra-state sale of goods and services wherein this transaction takes place.
  For instance, as in the above example, the business supplies iron ore from Maharashtra to a consumer in West Bengal. The GST, thus collected, is divided between the central government and the 'West Bengal government' (State of consumption).

> State GST (state tax/SGST) would be called UTGST (Union Territory Goods and Services Tax) in Union territories without a legislature. CGST. *As discussed earlier, CGST & SGST/UTGST shall be levied on all taxable intra-state supplies.*

- **IGST (Integrated Goods and Services Tax)** is collected by the central government for inter-state sale of goods and services. IGST will also be applicable on the import and export of goods.

  The IGST is CGST plus SGST on all inter-state supply of goods or services or both. The inter-state supplier will pay IGST on value addition after adjusting the available credit of IGST, CGST and SGST on his purchases. The 'exporting state' will transfer to the centre the credit of SGST used in payment of IGST. The person based in the 'destination state' will claim credit of IGST while discharging his output tax liability in his own state. The centre will transfer to the 'importing state' the credit of IGST used in payment of SGST.[2]

In the GST regime, the tax structure will be as shown in Table 10.1.

Table 10.1 Tax structure under GST

Transaction	*Tax*	*Revenue sharing*
Sale within the state	CGST + SGST	Revenue will be shared equally between the centre and the state
Sale to another state	IGST	There will only be one type of tax (central) in the case of inter-state sales. The centre will then share the IGST revenue based on the destination of goods

Illustration 10.1: Dealer 'A' in Rajasthan sells the goods to dealer 'B' in Rajasthan worth Rs. 10,000. Further, dealer 'B' in Rajasthan resells goods to dealer 'C' in Punjab for Rs. 20,000. Finally, dealer 'C' in Punjab sells goods to end-consumer 'D' in Punjab for Rs. 25,000. GST @ 18% comprises SGST @ 9% and CGST @ 9%.

The tax implihcation at every stage is depicted as follows:

- In the above case, the dealer 'A' has to charge Rs. 1,800 as GST. Out of this, Rs. 900 will go to the central government and Rs. 900 will go to the Rajasthan government as the sale is 'within the state'.
- Then dealer 'B' will charge Rs. 3,600 from dealer 'C', which will go to the central government as the sale is 'inter-state'.
- Finally, dealer 'C' charges Rs. 4,500 as GST from the end-consumer. Out of this Rs. 2,250 revenue will go to the central government and Rs. 2,250 will go to the Punjab government as the sale is once again 'within the state'.

The tax settlement for the above is presented in Table 10.2. The GST tax implications are presented in Figure 10.4.

Advantages of GST

GST will have a multiplier effect on the economy, and its benefits in various forms and to different sectors are discussed below.

1 *Single tax.* By subsuming multiple taxes, GST has led to a harmonised system of indirect taxes. GST avoids the cascading effect of tax as the tax is calculated only on the value

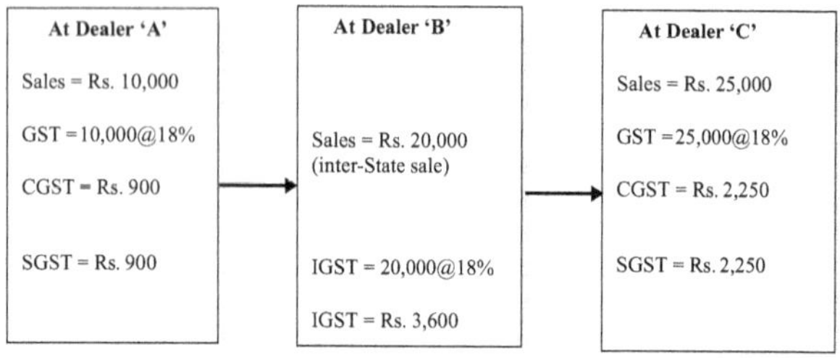

Figure 10.4 Tax implications under GST.

addition by persons whenever the ownership gets transferred, as discussed earlier.

2 *Lower cost of goods and services*. GST removes the cascading effect on the sale of goods and services, which directly impacts the cost of goods. Since tax on tax is eliminated in this process, the cost of goods decreases.

3 *Benefits to exporters*. GST reduces the cost of locally manufactured goods. This will increase the competitiveness of Indian goods in the international markets, thereby giving a boost to Indian exports.

Benefits of GST

GST offers multiple benefits to the Indian nation, as discussed earlier. The following is a snapshot of its benefits:

A. Indian economy

- Unified common national market for India
- Boost to foreign investment and 'Made in India' campaign
- Boost to exports
- Substantive economic growth
- Better employment opportunities
- Reduction in tax evasion
- Better compliance

B. Consumers

- Reduction in prices of goods and services
- Transparency in taxation system

C. Business houses/traders

- Single tax and reduction in multiplicity of taxes
- Simpler tax system
- Input tax credit
- Increase in exports

Key terminologies under GST

I. Taxable person

He is a person who carries out any business at any place in India and is registered or required to be registered under the GST Act.

Amongst others, GST registration is mandatory for:

- Any business whose turnover in a financial year exceeds Rs. 20 lakhs (Rs. 10 lakhs for North Eastern and hill states)
- An input service distributor
- An e-commerce operator or aggregator
- A person who supplies via an e-commerce aggregator
- An NRI doing business in India
- Other(s)

II. GSTN

The Goods and Services Tax Network (GSTN) has been set up by the government as a private company under Section 8 of the Companies Act, 2013. It would provide three front-end services to the taxpayers, namely registration, payment and return.

III. GSTIN

This refers to the unique 'GST identification number' that every business will be allotted. Every taxpayer will be allotted

Table 10.2 Tax statement under GST

Stage	*Parties*	*Sale Price (Rs.)*	*Tax Amount Received (Rs.)*				
			Rajasthan govt.	*Punjab govt.*		*Central govt.*	
I	A to B	10,000	10,000*9% = 900	–		10,000*9% = 900	
II	B to C	20,000	–	–		20,000*IGST @18%	3,600
						(-) CGST credit	900
						(-) SGST credit	900
						Net	**1,800**
III	C to D	25,000	–	25,000*SGST @9%	2,250	25,000*CGST @9%	2,250
				(-) IGST credit balance (3,600–2,250)	1,350	(-) IGST credit**	2,250
				Net	**900**	**Net**	0
Total Receipt			**900**	**900**		**2,700**	
IV	**Adjustment**		(-) 900 going to Centre	(+) 1,350 coming from Centre		(+) 1,350	
Final			0	2,250		2,250	

Notes:
1. ** IGST credit is applied to set off in this order:
   first set off against IGST liability, then CGST, and the balance credit is used to set off SGST.
2. GST being a consumption-based tax, the state where the goods were consumed (Punjab) will receive GST. So, Rajasthan (where goods were sold) will not get any taxes.
   Punjab government and central government will get (25,000*9%) = Rs. 2,250 each.
   Thus, Rajasthan (exporting state) will have to transfer credit of SGST of Rs. 900 (used in payment of IGST) to the Centre.
   In turn, the central government will transfer to Punjab (importing state) Rs. 1,350 IGST.

4 *Increased efficiency*. GST is mainly technologically driven. All activities like registration, return filing, application for refund and response to notice are done online on the GST Portal. This speeds up the processes.
5 *Higher collection*. This indirect tax system under GST improves the collection of taxes as well as boosts the development of the Indian economy by removing the indirect tax barriers between states and integrating the country through a uniform tax rate.
6 *Ease of doing business*. GST has resulted in a simpler tax regime, avoiding multiplicity of taxes and a reduction in the compliance cost. All interaction is through the common GSTN portal; therefore, less public interface between the taxpayer and the tax administration. This makes business in India easier and simpler.

a state-wise, PAN-based 15-digit Goods and Services Taxpayer Identification Number.

IV. *Reverse charge*

Generally, when the supplier supplies goods, the tax is levied upon the supplier. In certain cases, the tax is levied upon the buyer of the goods. This is called 'reverse charge' as the chargeability of tax gets reversed. This is applicable on goods and services both.

V. *Composition scheme*

This is an alternative method of levying tax meant for small taxpayers with low turnover, that is, taxpayers whose aggregate turnover does not exceed Rs. 1.5 crores threshold in a financial year. In case of special category states, this limit is Rs. 75 lakhs. The objective of this scheme is to make compliance easier and cost-effective for the taxpayers.

GST composition scheme rate is given in Table 10.3.

VI. *E-way bill*

This refers to the electronic waybill or electronic permit required for the movement of goods throughout the country. This bill is required for both inter-state (between different states) and intra-state (within a state) movement of goods.

Table 10.3 GST composition scheme tax rate

Sl. no.	*Category of registered persons*	*Rate of tax*
1	Manufacturers of goods (other than those specifically notified by govt.)	2% of the turnover
2	Restaurant Services	5% of the turnover
3	Traders or Any other supplier eligible for composition levy	1% of the turnover

Source: Composition Levy, https://cbic-gst.gov.in/pdf/faq-manual/faq-composition-levy-revised.pdf (accessed on 9 October 2023).

Invoices under GST

There are two types of invoices under the new regime:

- Tax invoice
- Bill of supply

I. *Tax invoice*

This is issued by a registered supplier when supplying taxable goods or services. The following are the rules regarding the use and contents of the invoice:

- *Serial number of the invoice:* Serial numbers are consecutive and consist of letters, numbers, special characters or any combination thereof; they are unique for each financial year.
- *Billing and shipping address:* This information is required as it will ultimately determine the 'place of supply' and the taxation of such transaction accordingly.
- *GSTIN/unique ID:* A GST identification number is required for the receiver.
- *HSN code/accounting code:* The notified person must include an HSN code for the goods and an accounting code for the services supplied.

II. *Bill of supply*

The bill of supply is issued by a registered supplier when:

- The goods or services supplied are exempt
- The supplier decides to pay taxes under the composition scheme

The bill of supply must contain the following details:

- *Serial number:* It should be a consecutive number consisting of letters and/or numbers and should be unique for one financial year.

- *Details of receiver:* These are required only if the receiver is registered – name, address and GSTIN/unique ID of the receiver.
- *Particulars of goods:* The value of the supply of goods or services or both, taking into account discount or abatement.

References

1 Times of India, June 30, 2025, https://timesofindia.indiatimes.com/business/india-business/double-in-just-5-years-gross-gst-collections-hit-record-high-of-rs-22–08-lakh-crore-in-fy25-average-monthly-number-at-rs-1–84-lakh-crore/articleshow/122159186.cms (accessed on 16 August 2025).
2 Goods and Services Tax (GST). 'Concept & Status', pp. 8, 35–37, https://gstcouncil.gov.in/sites/default/files/GST-Concept%20and%20Status01062019.pdf (accessed on 9 October 2023).

Glossary

Acquisition It refers to acquiring of effective working control by one company over another.

Alternate Minimum Tax (AMT) This is the minimum tax made applicable to all other taxpayers except companies.

Amalgamation (or consolidation) This implies that all the firms are combined to form a new entity through the transfer of all their property to such a new corporation.

American Depositary Receipts (ADRs) These depositary receipts are issued by non-US companies to raise capital in the US equity market from US investors.

Assessee This means a person by whom any tax or any other sum of money is payable under the Income Tax Act, 1961.

Assessment Year This is the year in which income is taxable and refers to the period of 12 months starting from April 1 and ending on March 31 of the next year.

Asset Management Companies (AMCs) These are the companies that operate the mutual funds.

Backward Integration This is when a company combines with the supplier of material.

Balanced Mutual Funds These funds invest in a mix of equities and fixed income securities.

Bank Finance It refers to the finance raised from commercial banks.

Bank Rate: It is the rate of interest that a central bank charges on loans and advances to a commercial bank.

Bid Rate The buying rate in the forex market is known as the 'bid rate'.

Bills of Exchange (or discounted bills) These are short-term, negotiable and liquidating instruments with low risk.

Book Value per Share (BV) It measures the net worth to be enjoyed by the ordinary shareholders of the company after all debts are paid.

Borrowed Funds They refer to the borrowings of a business firm.

Call Money It is the money lent by a bank that is repayable on demand.

Call Option It gives the buyer the right but not the obligation to buy a certain quantity of the underlying asset, at a given price on or before the specified date in the future.

Capital Market (or stock market) It is a market for long-term funds, that is, funds of more than one year.

Catastrophic Bond They are the bonds whose performance is linked to some catastrophic incident.

CCIL The Clearing Corporation of India Ltd. (CCIL) was set up on the initiative by RBI to provide guaranteed clearing and settlement functions for transactions in money, G-Secs, foreign exchange and derivative markets.

Central Board of Direct Taxes (CBDT) This provides inputs for policy and planning of direct taxes in India and is responsible for the administration of direct tax laws through the Income Tax Department.

Central Board of Indirect Taxes & Customs (CBIC) This is responsible for the formulation of policy concerning the levy and collection of customs, GST, central excise, service tax and narcotics in India and their administration.

Central Goods and Services Tax (CGST) This is collected by the central government on an intra-state sale of goods and services.

Certificate of Deposits (CODs) A short-term bank deposit.

Close-Ended Mutual Funds These are funds with a pre-specified life and are redeemable at the end. These are listed in the stock exchanges and traded like stocks.

Commercial Paper (CPs) Commercial Paper is a short-term, unsecured debt instrument note issued by corporate and financial institutions at a discounted price.

Composition Scheme An alternative method of levying tax meant for small taxpayers with low turnover, that is, taxpayers whose aggregate turnover does not exceed Rs. 1.5 crores threshold in a financial year.

Conglomerate Merger This is a combination of two or more firms that are engaged in unrelated lines of business activity.

Convertible Debentures These debentures are convertible into shares after a specified period of time.

Convertible Preference Shares These preference shares are convertible into equity shares after a specified period of time.

Corporate Governance It is the system by which businesses are directed and controlled.

Cost of Debt It is an explicit cost in the form of interest paid by the company on the loan amount.

Cost of Equity Capital (COCE) It is an implicit cost as there is no assured/coupon rate of return involved here. It is the rate of return that the firm must earn to meet shareholders' expectations and thereby increase shareholders' wealth.

Cumulative Fixed Deposits These are the deposits where the interest accumulates with principal, earning higher returns compared to a non-cumulative plan.

Cumulative Preference Shares These preference shares are those where dividend is accumulated and paid in total if not paid in a specific year.

Debentures (or bonds) They are known as creditorship securities because debenture holders are the creditors of a company.

Depository Receipts These are owned securities of domestic companies issued in a foreign country in its currency.

Derivatives These are instruments whose value is derived from the price of some underlying asset like securities, commodities, bullion, currency, interest level, stock market index and so forth.

Direct Quotations The exchange quotation that gives the price for a foreign currency in terms of the domestic currency.

Direct Tax It is a tax that is levied directly on individuals and corporate entities and cannot be transferred to others.

Discounted Cash-Flow Method of Valuation (DCF) It attempts to determine the value of the company by computing the present value of cash flows over the life of the company. It is widely used in capital investment decisions.

Economic Value Added (EVA) It is the financial performance measure that captures the true economic profit of an enterprise. It is the profits generated by any economic entity over its COCE.

Economic Value Method of Human Valuation (or discounted net present value of future earnings method). Under this method, human asset is valued on the basis of the contribution they will make to the organisation till their retirement from the job.

Embedded Finance (EmFi) It is a concept that typically allows non-financial entities to integrate financial services/ products into their own platform.

Enterprise Value Method of Valuation The 'enterprise value' is the total of value of equity and debt minus cash and cash equivalents.

Equity-Linked Saving Schemes (ELSS) They are equity mutual funds that are qualified for tax exemption under Section 80C of the Income Tax Act.

Equity Shares (or ordinary shares or common shares) These are those shares that do not carry any special or preferential rights in the payment of annual dividend or repayment of capital.

E-Way Bill The Electronic Way Bill or electronic permit is required for the movement of goods exceeding Rs. 50,000 in value.

Financial Market It is a marketplace where buyers and sellers come together and take part in the trade of assets, such as equities, bonds and derivatives.

Financial Synergies These are the synergies that increase the capacity of the combined firm to mobilise financial resources at a lower cost.

Fintech It refers to the use of technology to enhance or automate financial services and processes.

Forex Market The forex market, or 'foreign exchange market', is the market that brings the participants across the globe together to buy, sell, exchange and speculate on currencies.

Forwards A forward contract is a contract between two parties, where settlement takes place on a specific date in the future at today's pre-agreed price.

Forward-Forward Swap Here, both the deals are in the forward, that is, one buys two months forward and sells three months forward, each deal cancelling the other or vice versa.

Forward Integration It is when a firm combines with the buyer or customer.

Forward Market It is the place where the transactions for the exchange of currencies take place at a specified future date after the spot date.

Futures A future is a contract between two parties to buy or sell an asset in the future at a specific price.

Global Depositary Receipts (GDRs) These represent depository receipts issued outside the US.

Goods and Services Tax (GST) An 'indirect tax' that has replaced many central and state indirect taxes levied on goods and services in India.

Goods and Services Tax Network (GSTN) It has been set up by the government as a private limited company under Section 8 of the Companies Act, 2013, to provide three front-end services to the taxpayers, namely registration, payment and return.

Government Securities (G-Secs) They refer to government and semi-government debt securities issued by the RBI.

Growth Mutual Funds These predominantly invest in equities. These funds aim to grow faster than other funds, so there is usually a higher risk.

GST Identification Number (GSTIN) This refers to the unique PAN-based, 15-digit Goods and Services Taxpayer Identification Number.

Historical Cost Method of Human Valuation Under this method, all actual costs incurred on recruitment, training, selection and so forth are capitalised. Then, the capitalised cost is amortised (writ- ten off) over the period an employee serves in the organisation.

Holding Company It is the parent company that owns 20% or more shares of another company.

Horizontal Merger This is a combination or joining of two or more firms in the same area of business.

Human Resource Valuation (HRV) (or human resource accounting [HRA]) It is the process of identifying and measuring data about human resources and communicating this information to interested parties.

Income Mutual Funds These are primarily a debt fund. They invest in securities that pay a fixed rate of return, like government bonds and corporate bonds.

Index Mutual Funds These funds invest in a specific set of stocks of an index like the BSE Sensex or the NSE Nifty.

Indirect Quotations The exchange quotation that gives the quantity of foreign currency per unit of domestic currency.

Indirect Taxes These taxes are indirectly levied on the public through goods and services.

Industry-Specific Mutual Funds They focus upon specific industries, such as construction, pharmaceuticals or banking.

Inorganic Growth (or external growth) It is accomplished through various business combinations, namely, mergers and acquisitions (M&A).

Institutional Finance It refers to the finance raised from financial institutions, both central and state-level financial institutions.

International Financial Reporting Standards (IFRS) These are global standards for the preparation of financial statements by public companies as part of harmonisation of global reporting.

Intangible Fixed Assets These fixed assets are those that are not visible.

Integrated Goods and Services Tax (IGST) This is collected by the central government for the inter-state sale of goods and services.

Inter-Corporate Deposits (ICDs) These are usually an unsecured inter-corporate loan.

Irredeemable Debentures These debentures are issued for perpetuity.

Irredeemable Preference Shares These preference shares are issued for perpetuity.

Joint Hindu Family Business It may be defined as a form of business organisation in which all the male members of a Hindu undivided family carry on business under the management and control of the head of the family, called 'Karta'.

Joint Sector Enterprise It consists of those business undertakings wherein the ownership, management and control are shared jointly by the government, private entrepreneurs and the public.

Joint Stock Company It is an association of persons having a separate legal existence, perpetual succession and common seal and incorporated under the Companies Act, 1956.

Lev and Schwartz Model of Human Valuation It values human resources in the form of discounted present values of all future payments to the employees. Here, 'the human resource of a company is the summation of value of all the net present value (NPV) of expenditure on employees'.

Long-term Finance It refers to that category of funds whose repayment is generally more than a ten-year period.

Market Value Added (MVA) It is the market value created by the firm over its capital employed.

Market Value Method of Valuation (MV) It is presumed to reflect the public information about the company and its industry; it values the company as per the current price prevailing in the market.

Masala Bonds These are bonds issued outside India but denominated in Indian rupees, rather than the local currency of that country.

Medium-term Finance (or intermediate-term finance) It is that category of finance whose repayment can be projected within a planning cycle of a reasonable length of time.

Merger It refers to a fusion between two or more enterprises, which results in the emergence of a single enterprise.

Merged Company (or the transferee company) This is the company to which assets are transferred.

Merging Company (or the transferor company) These are the companies that transfer their assets to the other company.

Minimum Alternate Tax (MAT) The minimum tax to be paid by the companies.

Money Market It is a market for short-term funds, that is, funds up to one year.

Money Market Mutual Funds These funds invest in short-term fixed income securities, such as treasury bills, commercial paper and certificates of deposit.

Mutual fund It is a pool of money mobilised from numerous investors and invested on their behalf in several securities in the market.

National Anti-Profiteering Authority (NAPA) This is a body constituted under the GST by the central government to examine the complaints of non-passing the benefit of reduced tax incidence.

Neobanks They are essentially banks without any physical branch locations.

Net Assets Method of Valuation Under this, the total value of the assets (minus the liabilities) of the target company is computed to find out the value of the equity of its business.

Net Asset Value (NAV) Net asset value of a fund is the total of the market value of the assets (securities) that comprise its portfolio, net of any liabilities at that time. Net asset value of a unit is the NAV of the fund divided by the number of units outstanding.

Net Operating Profit after Tax (NOPAT) It is the profits generated from the core operations of the company after tax.

Net Present Value (NPV) It is the difference between the present value of net cash inflows and the present value of cash outflows.

Non-Convertible Debentures These debentures are not convertible into equity shares.

Non-Convertible Preference Shares These preference shares are those that are not convertible into equity shares.

Non-Cumulative Fixed Deposits These deposits pay off the interest earned on investment on a regular basis.

Non-Cumulative Preference Shares These preference shares do not have a cumulative advantage of dividend.

Offer Rate The selling rate in the forex market is known as the 'offer rate'.

Open-Ended Mutual Funds They are irredeemable and open for investment and redemption throughout the year.

Operating Synergies These are the synergies that result in economies of scale due to an increase in the scale of operations of the combined firm.

Opportunity Cost Method of Human Valuation This method is used to value those employees who possess specific skills and, thus, are rare in availability. A 'bid price' is offered by the managers for acquiring such scarce employees. This bid price becomes the investment in such employees.

Options An option gives the contract holder the right to buy or sell on a specified date in the future, but they are under no obligation.

Organic Growth It is increasing the profit base of the organisation through the capital investment process.

Over-The-Counter Market (OTC Market) An 'over-the-counter market' means that there is no single market or stock exchange but an electronic market where trading takes place.

Owned Funds They refer to the funds provided by the owners.

Permanent Account Number (PAN) A ten-digit unique alphanumeric number issued by the Income Tax Department in the form of a laminated plastic card.

Person The term 'person' includes an individual, a Hindu undivided family, a company, a firm, an association of persons or a body of individuals, a local authority, and every artificial juridical person.

Preference Shares These shares carry certain special or preferential rights in the payment of dividends and repayment of capital as compared to equity shareholders.

Previous Year The year in which income is earned. Also, 'the financial year immediately preceding the assessment year'.

Price to Book Ratio (P/B) It is a valuation ratio expressed as a multiple (i.e., how many times a company's stock is trading per share as compared to the company's book value per share).

Price to Earnings Ratio (P/E Multiple) It is a market prospect ratio that calculates the market value of a stock relative to its earnings.

Primary Market (or new issue market) It is a market that refers to the first-time issue of securities, that is, 'Initial Public Offering (IPO)'.

Private Placement It is the process by which securities are issued to selected mature and sophisticated institutional investors as opposed to the general public.

Public Deposits They refer to the deposits received by a company from the public as loans or debts.

Put Option It gives the buyer the right, but not the obligation, to sell a certain quantity of the underlying asset at a given price on or before the specified date.

Redeemable Debentures These debentures are repaid within the lifetime of the company.

Redeemable Preference Shares These preference shares are refundable during the lifetime of the company.

Replacement Cost Method of Human Valuation This method values the human resource on the basis of his replacement cost, that is the cost of recruitment, training and development, opportunity cost for the period till the new recruit attains the same efficiency level as the old (to be replaced) employee.

Repo Rate It is the rate at which banks can acquire funds from RBI by selling the securities and at the same time agreeing to repurchase them at a later date at a predetermined price.

Reserve Bank of India (RBI) It is the apex bank of India and regulates banking and financial companies in India.

Reverse Charge It is the tax levied upon the buyer of the goods.

Reverse Repo Rate It is the rate that is paid by the RBI to banks on the deposit of funds with the RBI.

Rights Issue It is the process when securities are exclusively offered to the existing shareholders.

Secondary Market It is a market that refers to the trading of existing securities.

Secured Debentures These debentures are secured against the assets of the company.

Secured Loan It is the loan taken by a company against an asset as security.

Securities and Exchange Board of India (SEBI) It is the stock market regulator of India.

Share It is one of the units into which the share capital of a company can be divided.

Shareholders Wealth Maximisation (SWM) Wealth maximisation is a combination of regular return to shareholders in the form of dividends and appreciating market returns.

Short-term Finance It is that category of finance that is employed by an enterprise for day-to-day operations.

Spot-Forward Swap In this swap, one deal is done in the spot market and another in the forward market, that is, one buys in the spot and sells in the forward or vice versa.

Spot Market It is the market where transactions for the exchange (purchase and sale) of currencies take place two days after the date of the contract.

Spread In the forex market, the difference between the 'bid rate' and the 'offer rate' is the gross profit for the bank and is known as the spread.

State Goods and Services Tax (SGST) This is collected by the state government on an intra-state sale of goods and services.

Stock Exchange These are marketplaces where buyers and sellers come together to trade in a firm's shares and other securities.

Swap Market It is a combination of a spot and a forward transaction. The term 'swap' implies a temporary exchange of one currency for another with an obligation to reverse it at a specific future date.

SWIFT It is an acronym for 'Society for Worldwide Interbank Financial Telecommunications'. It is a communications network for international financial market transactions that links effectively more than 25,000 financial institutions throughout the world that have been allotted bank-identified codes.

Synergies This refers to the value addition to the new entity due to combination of two separate companies.

Systematic Investment Plan (SIP) It involves investing a fixed amount in a mutual fund at regular intervals, monthly or quarterly, over a period of time, thereby averaging out the cost of investing and yielding the benefit from the power of compounding.

Takeover A 'forced' acquisition is called a takeover.

Tax Deduction and Collection Account Number (TAN) A ten-digit alphanumeric number required to be obtained by all persons who are responsible for deducting or collecting tax.

Taxable Person A person who carries out any business at any place in India and is registered or required to be registered under the GST Act.

Term Loans These are long-term loans provided by central and state-level financial institutions to business firms.

Treasury Bills (T-bills) These are short-term government securities issued by the RBI on behalf of the central government.

Two-Way Quotations It means the rate quoted by the bank will indicate two prices, one at which it is willing to buy the foreign currency, and the other at which it is willing to sell the foreign currency.

Unsecured Debentures These are simple debentures and have no security.

Unsecured Loan It is a loan taken by a company without any security.

Value-Added Tax (VAT) A consumption tax levied on a product whenever value is added at each stage of the supply chain, from production to the point of sale.

Value Creation It is a corporation's raison d'être, the ultimate measure by which it is judged.

Vertical Merger This is a combination of two or more firms involved in different stages of the production or distribution.

Weighted Average Cost of Capital (WACC) (or COCE) It is the total cost of raising the funds for investment purposes.

Zero-coupon Bonds (or deep discount bonds) These bonds are issued at a substantial discount but redeemed at full.

Index

Note: Page locators in *italic* indicate a figure, and page locators in **bold** indicate a table on the corresponding page.

For Product Safety Concerns and Information please contact our EU representative GPSR@taylorandfrancis.com
Taylor & Francis Verlag GmbH, Kaufingerstraße 24, 80331 München, Germany

www.ingramcontent.com/pod-product-compliance
Lightning Source LLC
LaVergne TN
LVHW021129300926
849160LV00010B/929
* 9 7 8 1 0 4 1 2 2 0 1 1 4 *